S0-BDA-740

HIDDEN PICTURE-PERFECT
escapes

Palm Springs

PICTURE-PERFECT
escapes

Palm Springs

Richard Mahler

photographed by
Margaux Gibbons

Ulysses Press

Text Copyright © 2005 Ulysses Press. All rights reserved, including the right to reproduce this book or portions thereof in any form or by any means, electronic or mechanical, including photocopying, recording, or by any information storage or retrieval system, without written permission from the publisher, except for use by a reviewer in connection with a review.

Published by: Ulysses Press
                P.O. Box 3440
                Berkeley, CA 94703
                www.ulyssespress.com

ISBN 1-56975-431-4
ISSN 1551-4838

Printed in Canada by Transcontinental Printing

10 9 8 7 6 5 4 3 2 1

Interior photo credits: © Margaux Gibbons except for credits indicated on page 213
Cover photographs: large front photo of Indian Canyons by Arthur Coleman Photography, compliments of Palm Springs Bureau of Tourism. All other cover photos © Margaux Gibbons
Design: Sarah Levin, Leslie Henriques
Editorial and production: Lynette Ubois, Claire Chun, Lee Micheaux, Steven Schwartz, Lily Chou, Laura Brancella, Leona Benten
Maps: Pease Press
Index: Sayre Van Young

Distributed in the United States by Publishers Group West and in Canada by Raincoast Books

Ulysses Press 🐢 is a federally registered trademark of BookPack, Inc.

The authors and publisher have made every effort to ensure the accuracy of information contained in *Hidden Picture-Perfect Escapes Palm Springs*, but can accept no liability for any loss, injury, or inconvenience sustained by any traveler as a result of information or advice contained in this guide.

WRITE TO US

If in your travels you discover a spot that captures the spirit of Palm Springs, or if you live in the region and have a favorite place to share, or if you just feel like expressing your views, write to us and we'll pass your note along to the author.

We can't guarantee that the author will add your personal find to the next edition, but if the writer does use the suggestion, we'll acknowledge you in the credits and send you a free copy of the new edition.

ULYSSES PRESS
P.O. Box 3440
Berkeley, CA 94703
E-mail: readermail@ulyssespress.com

TABLE OF CONTENTS

Maps

1.
Palm Springs
and Beyond

East of Los Angeles lies a paradoxical land of brilliant greens and dusty browns, scorched flats and snow-thatched peaks. The Coachella Valley, a mere two-hour drive from Hollywood, is quintessential Southern California. It's a place where a motivated visitor can play a round of golf, explore a palm-shaded canyon, soak in a hot spring, enjoy a gourmet meal, and attend a symphony concert—all in the same day.

Little wonder that the region's unofficial capital, Palm Springs, is a refuge for the rich, the famous, the retired, and the over-worked. Here restoration and reinvention are not only possible, they are encouraged. Among those who seek solace in this sybaritic oasis, sensory pleasures and recreational pastimes are elevated to a fine art.

Only 400 feet above sea level, Palm Springs nestles beneath an imposing mountain range that soars nearly two miles high. Despite its stark surroundings, this sun-drenched town is a lush, tree-shaded community of flower-adorned gardens, broad lawns, and ornate fountains. Today this city and its neighbors are a golfer's paradise, with over 110 courses available and many tournaments held each year. In addition, the region boasts scores of tennis courts, dozens of bike trails, and one swimming pool per every five residents. Together with the smaller satellite towns of Cathedral City, Rancho Mirage, Palm Desert, Indian Wells, and La Quinta, Palm Springs is an opulent enclave in which billboards are prohibited, buildings are limited to heights of 30 feet, and bougainvillea are more common than cacti.

Palm Springs lies at the western end of a wide basin created by earthquake faults that over the millennia have dropped the eastern end of the Coachella Valley to well below sea level. Here a vast saltwater lake called the Salton Sea occupies hundreds of square miles of the Colorado Desert, America's hottest, driest landscape. Wedged between the Salton

Sea and metropolitan Palm Springs are huge tracts of farmland, made productive through irrigation, fertilizer, and year-round warmth. The surrounding mountains block most rain, creating a climate that is ideal for growing dates, citrus, tomatoes, peppers, and other heat-loving crops.

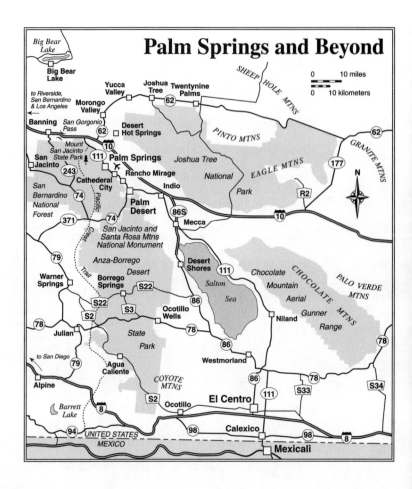

The area's year-round sunshine is the foundation of its tourism as well. The almost completely dry winter, with daily highs in the 70s and 80s, attracts pale snowbirds from the north and east, along with weary urbanites from the west and south. These visitors join a growing number of full-time inhabitants who revel in the balmy atmosphere.

Although the city already had been home to several small resorts, due to its hot springs and warm climate, silent-era movie stars Ralph Bellamy and Charlie Farrell often are credited with turning Palm Springs into Hollywood's favorite playground. In 1930, the tennis-playing actors began buying up desert land at $30 an acre and built a sumptuous hotel and racquet club that attracted Humphrey Bogart, Ginger Rogers, Clark Gable, and other luminaries. Famous folks were attracted to Palms Springs by its warm weather, proximity to Los Angeles, and tolerant attitude. Here the rich and famous could do what they pleased—or nothing at all—without interference or fear of consequences.

During the 1950s and '60s, headliners like Bob Hope, Frank Sinatra, Liberace, Elvis Presley, Marilyn Monroe, and Kirk Douglas strengthened the resort city's chic cachet, which continues with a series of fresh celebrity faces to this day.

The Agua Caliente Indians inhabited the area originally and made the best of the desert's hidden

Moorten Botanical Gardens

charms, including its still-inviting natural mineral baths and thick palm groves. These American Indians hunted game in the surrounding mountains and sustained themselves for an estimated 3000 years through the wise use of food-producing plants and abundant springs. The Agua Calientes and neighboring bands of Cahuilla Indians were largely ignored by the Spanish and Mexican settlers who colonized California during the 18th and 19th centuries, allowing their indigenous culture and homeland to remain largely intact.

During the late 1800s, however, the United States government divided much of the territory into a checkerboard, giving odd-numbered square sections of land to the Southern Pacific Railroad and deeding the rest to the Agua Calientes. Today much of this valuable property is leased by the Indians to tourist resorts, retail stores, and individual homeowners under long-term contracts.

The actual hot-water springs from which Palm Springs gets its name has been diverted into a modern vacation complex operated by the tribe. Dozens of other lavish resorts here are hidden among world-class golf courses, boutique shopping districts, and upscale neighborhoods. With so many resorts to choose from, a variety of specialized options have sprung up, including clothing-optional, family-friendly, gay-only, plastic surgery–providing, and health-oriented getaways.

About ten miles north of Palm Springs is Desert Hot Springs, a sprawling, low-rise tourist town that has long been the downscale alternative to its chic neighbor. Although that's changing gradually, it's still a community where visitors on a modest travel budget can feel comfortable.

Driving east of Palm Springs along the busy Route 111 corridor, travelers pass through a series of interconnected communities, each with its fair share of visitor attractions. One can't help but notice the obvious prosperity of these fast-growing cities, where new construction projects are as ubiquitous as the established walled-in homes that have provided comfort and privacy for a generation of prominent American power brokers, opinion shapers, and entertainers.

Unpretentious Cathedral City, nicknamed "Cat City" by locals, is known for its fun resale stores and a celebrity cemetery shared by Frank Sinatra and Sonny Bono. Next door is affluent Rancho Mirage, where the area's golf craze started in the 1940s and lives on at mega-resorts surrounded by water hazards and fairways. In the kind of surreal juxtaposi-

tion that is considered normal here, the city also
encompasses the Betty Ford drug rehab center, a
children's museum, a Vegas-style casino, and a huge
shopping center perched on a fake river.

Mary Pickford Theater & Salon

An up-and-coming arts center, Palm Desert is
home to the region's finest galleries and most lavish performance venue. It is also a shopper's unchallenged nirvana, with its own requisite super-
mall as well as a classy flea market and a mile-long
street jammed with boutiques and specialty stores.
The valley's most fashionable residential address lies

Where Does All the Water Come From?

First-time Palm Springs visitors are surprised—sometimes even appalled—at the indiscriminate use of water in one of North America's driest deserts. Unlike drought-plagued areas of the West, where water conservation is mandated by law as well as by conscience and custom, the Coachella Valley is a land where golf courses, decorative fountains, swimming pools, artificial lakes, non-native plants, and water-misters are the norm. This is possible only because a huge natural aquifer stores an estimated 200-year supply of water underground. Over millennia, the basin's sandy soil has collected moisture from rain and snow falling on nearby mountains. In addition, the Colorado River has occasionally shifted its course, inundating the Coachella Valley for months at a time. But having confirmed that the water table is, in fact, dropping rapidly, some experts believe the aquifer is being depleted too quickly. Efforts are underway to conserve usage, but until the warnings of hydrologists are heeded it appears that water use in the area will remain largely unrestricted.

farther along Route 111 in Indian Wells, where opulent houses are the norm and tennis vies with golf as the pastime of choice. In neighboring La Quinta, the emphasis is on luxury resorts hidden from common view by acres of lush courses designed by celebrity golfers. Unlike Indian Wells, La Quinta is also a retail center, with an "old town" shopping district filled with one-of-a-kind stores and charming restaurants. Modest Indio, the most easterly link in the suburban chain, is a home base for young families and singles. This sprawling town is a true palm oasis, with date orchards reaching from roads' edge to the mountains.

A short drive north of all this hubbub, serene Joshua Tree National Park lies astride the Low and High deserts, rising from the scorching Colorado to the cooler climes and higher elevations of the Mojave. Noted for its impressive cacti, oddly shaped boulders, and dense stands of Joshua trees, this uninhabited preserve was formerly home to the Chemehuevi Indians.

PACKING AND PREPARATION

There are two important guidelines when deciding what to take on a trip. The first is as true for Palm Springs as anywhere in the world—pack light. Lifestyles here are relaxed and casual, with few opportunities for dressing up,

so there's no need to bring a lot of luggage. You may also want to take advantage of the many fine retailers in the area that sell clothing. Remember that the airlines allow two suitcases, one carry-on bag, and one "personal item" for no extra charge.

The second rule is to prepare for temperature variations. While winter daytime highs often hover in the 80s or even 90s, evenings can bring lows in the 40s and 50s. A light sweater, jacket, long-sleeved shirt, and pants are advisable from November through March, in addition to the *de rigueur* shorts and T-shirts. You may wish to bring a raincoat if you're planning to visit from December to February—when even Palm Springs gets an occasional cool shower—and if you're traveling in the high mountains during winter, carry cold-weather clothing. Mountain temperatures are usually at least 20 degrees lower than on the valley floor. If you come during summer, be aware that Palm Springs can be fiercely hot, with daytime temperatures from May through September often topping 100 degrees and night-time lows dipping only into the 70s or 80s. Thunderstorms occasionally occur during summer, but rainfall is brief and spotty. The saving grace of Palm Springs year-round is its low humidity, predictable sunshine, and frequent breezes.

LODGING

Overnight accommodations in Palm Springs are as varied as the region itself. They range from posh resorts and exclusive spas to retro-hip motels and cozy bed-and-breakfast inns. You're bound to find something here to fit your budget and taste, including the nationwide chains, though the emphasis in Palm Springs is definitely on higher-priced, more luxurious accommodations.

My personal preference is for historic properties, those sometimes slightly faded classics that combine charm, service, and tradition at moderate cost. I also suggest smaller inns and bed and breakfasts as an opportu-

The Casual Dress Code

With the local economy built around outdoor recreation, Palm Springs-area restaurants not only accept but expect the majority of their diners to dress casually. Indeed, many customers arrive directly from the golf course or tennis court. Shorts, T-shirts, and sportswear are generally not out of place here. You'll want to dress up a bit when heading to more expensive restaurants, particularly for dinner, but very few expect a coat and tie for men or long dresses for women. If in doubt, call ahead or consult your hotel concierge.

nity to stay in a homelike setting where it's easy to glean insider tips about the area from knowledgeable employees as well as fellow travelers.

Choosing appropriate lodging is highly subjective and will ultimately depend on your taste, itinerary, and credit card limit. In order to help you pick a place to stay, I've organized accommodations not only by area but also according to price. Note that rates listed are for double-occupancy during the high season; prices often decrease by 40 to 70 percent in the low season, which in Palm Springs is generally May through September. If you don't mind the intense heat, bargains abound. During what is locally referred to as "The Season," January through April, rooms fill up quickly and you are advised to book as far in advance as possible.

Budget hotels generally are less than $60 per night for two people; the rooms are clean and comfortable, but not luxurious. The *moderate*-priced hotels run $60 to $120 and provide larger rooms, plusher furniture, and more attractive surroundings. At a *deluxe* hotel you can expect to spend between $120 and $175 for a double. You'll generally check into a spacious, well-appointed room after passing through a fashionable lobby, usually complemented by a restaurant, lounge, and cluster of shops. If you want to spend your time (and money) in one of the area's very finest hotels—try an *ultra-deluxe* facility, which will include all the amenities and cost more than $175 per night.

For information on the full range of accommodations available in the area, as well as other useful subjects, the **Palm Springs Bureau of Tourism** can assist travelers. ~ 777 North Palm Canyon Drive, Palm Springs, CA 92262; 760-778-8415, 800-927-7256; www.palm-springs.org. Equally helpful (and serving nearby cities as well as Palm Springs) is the **Palm Springs Desert Resorts Convention and Visitors Bureau**. ~ 303 North Indian Canyon Drive, Palm Springs; 800-967-3767; www.desert-resorts.com.

DINING

Once something of a culinary desert (no pun intended), it now seems as if the Palm Springs area has more restaurants than people. In an attempt to create a pattern for this lively parade of places, I've organized them according to location and cost. Restaurants listed offer lunch and dinner unless otherwise noted. Within a particular chapter, dining places are categorized geographically, with

The Lively Gay & Lesbian Scene

Although Southern California is often stereotyped for its social and political conservatism, the tolerance that accompanies the booming entertainment industry makes certain areas particularly inviting for gay and lesbian travelers. Palm Springs is a place where hotels large, small, and in-between cater specifically and enthusiastically to gay and lesbian visitors. In fact many hostelries, along with a growing number of restaurants and shops, are gay- or lesbian-owned. The city government actively promotes gay-themed tourism and in late 2003 Palm Springs voters elected an openly gay mayor and two gay city councilors.

While in Palm Springs, consult the bimonthly publication, *MEGA-Scene*, for worldwide and local gay news as well as an extensive entertainment guide. ~ 611 South Palm Canyon Drive #7-B, Palm Springs; 760-327-5178, fax 760-323-3646; www.megasceneps.com. *The Bottom Line*, another bimonthly magazine, publishes a detailed roster of eateries, bars, hotels, and nightspots that gay travelers will find appealing. It also includes reviews of movies, books, and local theater. ~ 312 North Palm Canyon Drive, Palm Springs; 760-323-0552, fax 760-323-8400; www.psbottomline.com. For more information on gay- and lesbian-oriented events, entertainment, and activities, order the free, city-published *Palm Springs Gay & Lesbian Guide*. ~ 800-347-7746; www.palm-springs.org; or the independently published *Gay Yellow Pages of the Desert*. ~ 800-894-3203.

each entry describing the establishment as budget, moderate, deluxe, or ultra-deluxe in price.

Dinner entrées at *budget* restaurants usually cost $9 or less. The ambience is informal café-style. *Moderate*-priced restaurants range between $9 and $18 at dinner and offer pleasant surroundings, a more varied menu, and a slower pace. *Deluxe* establishments tab their entrées above $18, featuring sophisticated cuisines, plush decor, and more personalized service. *Ultra-deluxe* dining rooms, where $25 will only get you started, are gathering places in which cooking (one hopes) is a fine art form and impeccable service a way of life.

Breakfast and lunch menus vary less in price from one restaurant to another. Even deluxe kitchens usually offer light breakfasts and sandwiches at lunch, thus placing them within a few dollars of their budget-minded competitors. These early meals can be a good time to check out expensive restaurants.

CALENDAR OF LOCAL EVENTS

JANUARY Unspooling in Palm Springs and other locales, the **Palm Springs International Film Festival** features over 200 films from 60 countries.

Famous entertainers join golfing pros in Rancho Mirage for the annual **Bob Hope Desert Chrysler Golf Classic**.

FEBRUARY The **Riverside County Fair & National Date Festival**, held at the Indio Fairgrounds, features camel and ostrich races as well as an Arabian Nights pageant.

Founded as a charity benefit by the late singer, the **Frank Sinatra Celebrity Invitational Golf Tournament** is a crowd-pleaser, with both amateurs and entertainers teeing off in Palm Springs.

In Palm Springs, the **Tour de Palm Springs Bike Event** attracts cyclists from around the world to a course around the city and its environs.

MARCH Rancho Mirage hosts the **Kraft Nabisco Championship LPGA Golf Tournament**, formerly the Dinah Shore Golf Classic.

The **La Quinta Arts Festival** presents more than 250 fine artists in an outdoor sale and juried competition at the La Quinta Civic Center.

At Stevens Park in Palm Springs, the **Crossroads Renaissance Festival** recreates life in Elizabethan England, with emphasis on food, frolic, and games.

APRIL The four-day **White Party** is the area's biggest and best gay party of the year. The gala is part of a national White Party circuit that includes dancing, music, mixers, and, of course, parties, in Palm Springs attended by well over 25,000 visitors.

In Indian Wells, **Earth Day** is celebrated among the rare and beautiful flora and fauna inhabiting the Living Desert Museum.

MAY In Palm Springs, both the **Smooth Jazz Festival** and **Greater Palm Springs Celebrity Golf Classic** are celebrated at O'Donnell Golf Club.

The **Palm Springs Air Museum**, located at the city's airport, celebrates the contributions of military men and women to aviation with a series of special events, including a Memorial Day flower drop.

The **Coachella Valley Music and Arts Festival** is a multimedia experience featuring the best of the area's food, music, dancing, and art, based at the Empire Polo Grounds in Indio.

JUNE In Palm Springs, Camelot Theaters hosts the annual **Film Noir Festival**, focusing on rare, seldom-seen films of the '40s and '50s.

Elvis Presley "tribute artists" from all over the world gather in Palm Springs for **A Weekend With the King**, with prizes offered in various categories that memorialize the iconic singer.

Take Care in the Desert Air

What makes the desert an attractive travel destination can also make it deadly for those who venture out unprepared. Even during winter months, when the temperature can top 90 degrees, it's essential to remain properly hydrated. For many active visitors, this means drinking a gallon or more of water each day. And because uncontaminated water rarely occurs naturally in the desert, you must carry what you need when hiking or cycling. Hikers should avoid traveling alone and carry a cell phone if available, along with snacks, a bandanna, and a good map. The desert is also home to rattlesnakes and scorpions, both of which can cause injury. Hikers should consider wearing high-top shoes as a precaution against these animals and to protect themselves against sharp stones and thorns. If you're going far, bringing a whistle and electrolyte-laden drink is a good idea. A must for everyone, even on the golf course or tennis court, is a wide-brimmed hat and sunscreen.

JULY–AUGUST Palm Desert's **Summer of Fun** concert and movie series presents free family-oriented music and films under the stars on alternative Thursdays through July and August.

Fourth of July celebrations take place throughout the Coachella Valley, including fireworks, food, and patriotic entertainment at the Palm Springs Stadium.

SEPTEMBER **Rocktoberfest** draws classic-era rock music fans for free performances and parties in downtown Palm Springs.

High Desert vs. Low Desert

Joshua Tree generally receives between three and five inches of rain a year, with more falling at higher elevations, along with occasional snow. Hotter temperatures and stronger winds at lower levels cause moisture to evaporate more quickly. These factors combine to yield very different types of plants and animals from one section of the park to another. In the high desert, above 3000 feet, common desert plants include honey mesquite, catclaw acacia, Mojave yucca, and agave, along with the Joshua tree. Most

of these plants live for well over a century, and the agave has a lifespan of 600 to 1200 years. Stabilizing fragile soils that might otherwise blow or wash away, such tenacious plants also provide havens, food sources, and nests for animals. In the past, they were used by American Indians to make food, medicine, soap, and string as well as weavings and baskets. The low desert, below 3000 feet, has less vegetation overall, although the ocotillo puts on a colorful show from time to

time. The stick-like plant greens up after rainy periods and lipstick red flowers emerge from the ends of its branches. Also present here are cholla, palo verde, ironwood, creosote, and smoke trees. Palm trees are native to the lower elevations but several clusters survive outside their normal range in the park's highlands. Late winter and early spring are the best times to see wildflowers, which sometimes carpet both the high and low desert for as far as the eyes can see. The peak wildflower season is usually February through May; the park maintains a "wildflower hotline" (760-340-0435) where you can get up-to-date information about where and what is blooming.

Fall Concerts in Sunrise Park take place one evening a week from mid-September through mid-October in Palm Springs, with picnic suppers available.

Short-format films, videos, and cartoons are showcased at the **Palm Springs International Festival of Short Films**, the largest annual competition of its kind.

OCTOBER   American Heat: **Palm Springs Motorcycle & Hot Rod Weekend** draws thousands of motorcycle enthusiasts for a competition ride-in as well as music, stunts, games, and retail vendors.

The **Palm Springs Tramroad Challenge 6K** challenges hardy runners in a 2000-foot elevation-gain race up the road to the Tramway.

In Cabezon, the **Cabezon Band of Mission Indians** holds its annual powwow, with traditional food, music, and dancing offered to the public.

NOVEMBER   Imaginations run wild at **Rancho Mirage's Golf Cart Parade**, where scores of golf carts are whimsically transformed into everything from champagne bottles to slot machines, much to the delight of observers lined along El Paseo.

Greater Palm Springs **Gay Pride Weekend** celebrates gays and lesbians with a parade, art festival, food court, book-signings, music, and other offerings in downtown Palm Springs.

DECEMBER   The free, city-sponsored, two-day **Indio International Tamale Festival** attracts tens of thousands of visitors eager to sample dozens of delicious treats prepared by *tamaleros cocineros* (tamale-makers).

In Palm Springs, the annual **Festival of Lights Parade** brings the holiday mood to revelers on a pre-Christmas evening as thousands of lights adorn marching bands, floats, and equestrians along Palm Canyon Drive.

The **Greater Palm Springs Celebrity Golf Classic** is a tournament benefitting local youth charities, held in Indian Wells.

The **Desert Big Band and Jazz Party** brings straight-ahead jazz and big band music to Palm Springs at the Riviera Resort.

OUTDOOR ACTIVITIES

Averaging 330 days of sunshine annually, the Palm Springs area offers possibilities for outdoor recreation year-round. Summer's blast-furnace heat, however, can wilt even the most dedicated golfer by lunch and there are times when even a swimming pool may seem too hot. Accordingly, some businesses (including a significant number of hotels, stores, and restaurants) close down or reduce their hours during parts of June, July, and August. During fall and spring, however, and particularly during winter, milder temperatures and clear skies nearly guarantee perfect conditions for active visitors at any time, though debilitating hot spells also can occur in May and September.

Golf

Golfers in the Palm Springs area may think they've died and gone to heaven. The dozens of world-class courses here have attracted professionals and amateurs alike, including Bob Hope, Arnold Palmer, Lucille Ball, and former President Dwight Eisenhower. (Eisenhower recorded

Where to Get Golf Lessons

A number of reputable golf schools and clinics operate in the Coachella Valley, several of them based at golf courses or resorts. The best offer a combination of private instruction, small-group classes, course play, customized lessons, and video-based analysis. With direct access to two of the region's finest 18-hole courses, Indian Wells Golf School at the Golf Resort at Indian Wells is a good place for the beginner to learn the basics, or the advanced golfer to polish his or her skills. ~ 44-600 Indian Wells Lane, Indian Wells; 760-346-4653; www.golfatindianwells.com/golf school.asp.

Other options include Tahquitz Creek Golf Academy (760-328-1005) in Palm Springs; Cimarron Golf Academy (760-770-6060) in Cathedral City; College Golf Center (760-341-0994) at College of the Desert in Palm Desert; and Jim McLean Golf School (760-564-7144) at La Quinta Resort's PGA West.

his only hole-in-one on a Palm Springs fairway.) Enthusiasts are blessed with a wide range of attractive options throughout the Coachella Valley. Hotel concierges and booking agencies can help you determine which course is right for you, or you can make online reservations. ~ www.palmspringsteetimes.com. A complete course directory is also available. ~ www.desertgolfguide.com. A surprising amount of descriptive information is published in the local phone book.

Most facilities have carts for rent as well as driving ranges and other amenities. Greens fees typically run

PICTURE-PERFECT
Places to Tee Off

1. **PGA West in La Quinta,** *p. 29*
2. **Marriott Desert Springs in Palm Desert,** *p. 27*
3. **Westin Mission Hills Resort Golf Club in Rancho Mirage,** *p. 27*

from $100 to $200 during winter and spring. Rates are often higher on weekends or mornings, though you can still get on some public courses for $50 or less. In summer, many courses cut their fees in half. Last-minute tee times at discount prices can be arranged at many courses through **Stand-by Golf.** ~ 619-321-2665.

In early fall and late spring, some facilities close for a few weeks to change turf. Here's a select list of greens. (All those indicated below have 18 holes unless otherwise stated.)

PALM SPRINGS The **Tahquitz Creek Golf Resort** is open to the public and has two 18-hole courses, Resort and Legends. The 17th hole of the Resort's Ted Robinson–designed green boasts waterfalls and other unusual water hazards. Cart included. ~ 1885 Golf Club Drive; 760-328-1005. **Mesquite Golf and Country Club** has a course surrounded by mesquite trees and featuring spectacular mountain views. Cart included. ~ 2700 East Mesquite Avenue; 760-323-9377. Tommy Jacobs' **Bel Air Greens** has a 9-hole executive course and

driving range with relatively low fees. ~ 1001 South El Cielo Road; 760-322-6062.

DESERT HOT SPRINGS   Site of the 1999 Senior PGA Tour Qualifier, the 18-hole **Desert Dunes Golf Club** course was designed by Robert Trent Jones, Jr. ~ 19-300 Palm Drive; 760-251-5366. Ted Robinson designed the semiprivate, 18-hole **Mission Lakes Country Club** course, which has a driving range. ~ 8484 Clubhouse Boulevard; 760-329-8061.

CATHEDRAL CITY   Surrounded by mature olive and eucalyptus trees, the 18-hole executive course of the semiprivate **Date Palm Country Club** was designed by Ted Robinson. Closed October. ~ 36-200 Date Palm Drive; 760-328-1315. **Cathedral Canyon Country Club** is a semipublic facility with a driving range and three 9-hole courses. ~ 34-567 Cathedral Canyon Drive; 760-328-6571. **Cimarron Golf Resort** has two public, 18-hole courses, one long and one short. ~ 607-603 30th Avenue; 760-770-6060.

RANCHO MIRAGE At the **Westin Mission Hills Resort Golf Club**, two public choices are available. The Resort Course, a par 70 designed by Pete Dye, is considered difficult. ~ 71-501 Dinah Shore Drive; 760-328-3198. The **Gary Player Signature Course** is nearby. ~ 70-705 Ramon Road; 760-770-2908.

PALM DESERT The semiprivate **Desert Falls Country Club**, designed by Ronald Fream, is dotted with majestic palm trees and has a driving range. ~ 111 Desert Falls Parkway; 760-340-5646. The **Marriott Desert Springs Resort** offers two lush, par-72 courses designed by Ted Robinson: the Palms and the Valley. ~ 74-855 Country Club Drive; 760-341-1756. Across from the Marriott is **Desert Willow Golf Resort**, a self-described "environmentally sensitive" public facility with two courses that

Indian Wells Tennis Gardens

Since its opening in March 2000, the state-of-the-art Indian Wells Tennis Gardens has dominated the local tennis scene, attracting the sport's top players to its annual Pacific Life Open Tennis Tournament. Formerly the Tennis Masters Series Tournament, this world-class professional competition is the area's premiere event for tennis fans. The 16,000 seat facility offers viewers a chance to see the likes of Lindsay Davenport, Andy Roddick, Venus Williams, and Andre Agassi at the top of their games. Unfortunately, private play is restricted to members only. ~ City of Indian Wells, 760-345-8499, 800-999-1585; iwtg.net or www.pacificlifeopen.com.

Up, Up, and Away

For unmatched views of open desert terrain and surrounding mountains, there's nothing like a hot-air or gas-inflated balloon. Hour to hour-and-a-half-long rides are widely available during the winter season, some with a continental breakfast brunch on board and most including a champagne toast. **Desert Balloon Charters** offers two hour-long rides each day from late September through May. ~ La Quinta; 760-346-8575. **Balloon Above the Desert** operates September to May, with pickups at hotel or home. You can book on-line. ~ Palm Desert; 760-776-5785, 800-342-8506; www.pshotairballoons.com. From October to May, you can fly with **Dream Flights**. ~ Palm Desert; 760-346-5330, 800-933-5628; www.dreamflights.com. **Fantasy Balloon Flights** offers rides that include hotel pickups and champagne toasts. ~ Palm Desert; 760-568-0997, www.fantasyballoonflights.com.

use more sand and roughage than other clubs. ~ 38-955 Desert Willow Drive; 760-346-7060; www.desertwillow. com. At the semiprivate and modestly priced **Oasis Country Club**, fairways designed by David Rainville meander around 22 lakes and ponds. ~ 42-330 Casbah Way; 760-345-2715. To play with many tall palm trees swaying in the breeze, visit the semiprivate, par-72 **Palm Desert Resort Country Club**. ~ 77-333 Country Club Drive; 760-345-2781. The **Golf Center at Palm Desert** has a lighted driving range and an inexpensive 18-hole course, both open to the public. ~ 74-945 Sheryl Drive; 760-779-1877. Nestled against the Santa Rosa Mountains, the private **Bighorn Golf Club** has two meandering courses, designed by Ted Fazio and Arthur Hills. ~ 255 Palowet Drive; 760-341-4653.

INDIAN WELLS Both West and East courses at **The Golf Resort at Indian Wells** are designed by Ted Robinson, Sr., and have several lakes to keep the game interesting. ~ 44-5000 Indian Wells Lane; 760-346-4653.

LA QUINTA Another Pete Dye creation is the semiprivate TPC Stadium Course, one of the legendary greens at **PGA West**, part of La Quinta Resort & Club. Somewhat less challenging is the private Jack Nicklaus Tournament Course, designed by the famous golfer. Three other 18-hole courses here are championship level. ~ 50-200 Avenue Vista Bonita; 760-564-7686; www.laquinta resort.com, www.pgawest.com. The **Indian Springs Golf Course** is a modestly priced, 18-hole course with an all-grass practice facility. ~ 46-080 Jefferson Street; 760-775-3360.

INDIO The **Indio Municipal Golf Club** is a flat, public course with the longest par 3 in the nation. Attractions include a driving range, night lighting, and low cost. ~ 83-040 Avenue 42; 760-347-9156. Arthur Hills designed the **Heritage Palms Golf Club**'s 18-hole course,

Hitting the Ski Slopes

Skiing in the desert? Yes, even Palm Springs gives golfers and spa-goers a chance to challenge the surrounding slopes. The Palm Springs Aerial Tramway carries skiers to an elevation of over 8500 feet in the San Jacinto Mountains, where the **Adventure Center** rents cross-country gear and snowshoes. Ungroomed trails totaling 50 miles in length circle through backcountry wilderness. The required permit may be obtained at the ranger station near the tram stop. ~ 760-327-6002 (Adventure Center), 909-659-2607 (park information). Check ski conditions at 888-515-8726 or www.pstramway.com.

which is par 72. ~ 44-291 Heritage Palms Drive South; 760-772-7334. The two gently rolling courses at the **Landmark Golf Club**, North and South, are gorgeous. Request tee times online. ~ 84-000 Landmark Parkway; 760-775-2000; www.landmarkgc.com.

Tennis

Tennis, anyone? This is the sport that originally drew enthusiasts to the desert and there are plenty of opportunities in the area for aficionados, with a full range of courts, pro shops, and instructors to choose from.

In Palm Springs, city-owned **Demuth Park** offers four lighted courts. ~ 4375 Mesquite Avenue; 760-323-8272. Other options include **Ruth Hardy Park**, with eight courts. ~ Tamarisk Road and Avenida Caballeros. You'll

PICTURE-PERFECT
Desert Adventures

1. **Hiking in Palm Canyon,** *p. 38*
2. **Taking a hot-air balloon ride,** *p. 28*
3. **Cycling the bike trails of Palm Springs,** *p. 34*

find nine courts at **Plaza Raquet Club.** ~ 1300 Baristo Road; 760-323-8997.

In Palm Desert, **Marriott Desert Springs Resort** rents hard, clay, and grass courts to the public, with priority given to hotel guests. It's rated among the top 50 tennis resorts by *Tennis* magazine. ~ 74-855 Country Club Drive; 760-341-1893; www.marriotthotels.com/CTDCA. Palm Desert's **College of the Desert** also has six public courts. ~ 43-500 Monterey Avenue; 760-773-2591. **Wardman Park** features two lighted courts. ~ 66150 8th Street, Desert Hot Springs. The largest venue open to the public, on a limited basis, is at **Hyatt Grand Champions Resort** in Indian Wells, which hosts annual tournaments in its 11,500-seat stadium in addition to offering lighted courts, a ball machine, lessons, and a pro shop. ~ 44-650 Indian Wells Lane; 760-341-2582; www.grandchampions.hyatt.com. In Indio, there are two lighted public courts at **South Jackson Park.** ~ Jackson Street and Date Avenue. You may also try the four lighted courts at **Miles Avenue Park.** ~ Miles Avenue. **Indio High School** has six

Horsing Around

For those with their own horses, the **California Riding and Hiking Trail** runs 37 miles through Joshua Tree National Park, with several access points along the way. Camping with horses is allowed in the park at the Ryan and Black Rock campgrounds. Another 216 miles of trails are available throughout Joshua Tree, but not all of these have been marked or developed. Horses are welcome on dirt and paved roads, but not on nature trails.

lighted courts. ~ Avenue 46 and Clinton Avenue; 760-775-3550.

Remember, many resorts and country clubs have tennis courts available to their guests and members.

Horseback Riding

In Palm Springs, **Smoke Tree Stables** offers one-hour, two-hour, and day-long custom guided rides through stunning terrain, with routes featuring mountain, desert, and canyon views. No credit cards, reservations required. Closed July and August. ~ 2500 Toledo Avenue; 760-327-1372.

Covered Wagon Tours hosts two-hour pioneer-style desert tours on mule-drawn wagons, leading through the desert environment of Coachella Valley Preserve. A chuckwagon-style barbecue follows. Reservations required. Closed June through September. ~ La Quinta; 760-347-2161; www.coveredwagontours.com.

Rock Climbing

An increasingly popular sport in the Palm Springs area is rock climbing, particularly within Joshua Tree National

Park. The park's jumble of large granitic boulders and steep cliffs offer more than 5000 known rock-climbing routes, with many set up permanently for ascent by enthusiasts of all ages and abilities. Other rock-climbing adventures await in the San Jacinto Mountains and nearby foothills. Information about rock climbing within **Joshua Tree National Park** is available directly from the park. ~ 760-367-5500; www.nps.gov/jotr, e-mail jotr_info@nps.gov.

You can learn to rock climb or take guided climbing trips through **Uprising Adventure**, which runs half-, full-, and multi-day excursions in Joshua Tree National Park. All equipment is provided and all guides are AMGA certified. ~ P.O. Box 129, Joshua Tree 92252; 888-254-6266;

www.uprising.com, e-mail susancram@earthlink.net. Another experienced outfitter is **Vertical Adventures Rock Climbing School**, offering guides, trips, and classes in Joshua Tree. ~ P.O. Box 7548, Newport Beach, CA 92658; 800-514-8785, fax 949-854-5249; www.vertical-adven tures.com, e-mail bgvertical@aol.com.

Biking

Biking in the Palm Springs area is a rewarding experience for many visitors and some hotels provide bicycles to their guests at little or no charge. There are well-marked recreational routes through Palm Springs and outlying communities as well as off-road tracks in nearby canyons and parks. Joshua Tree is particularly well suited for mountain biking.

For those on road bikes, 35 miles of posted routes encircle the city of **Palm Springs**. Popular riding spots include the luxurious Tennis Club and Little Tuscany residential neighborhoods, the Mesquite Country Club area, Smoke Tree district, the Indian Canyons, and around local parks. Palm Springs routes are posted by the city on the Web. ~ www.palmsprings.com/city/palmsprings/bikemap.

One noteworthy trail is the ten-mile long **White Water Wash**, which begins in Palm Springs and extends into the city of Palm Desert. Check with bike shops for more tour information or pick up a bicycle-route map from **Palm Springs Leisure Center**. ~ 760-323-8272.

No trail or cross-country bicycling is allowed in **Joshua Tree**, but cyclists are welcome on paved and dirt roads open to vehicles. The recommended mountain bike routes include Queen Valley Road (easy), Geology Tour Road (moderate), and Pinkham Canyon Road (strenuous). Remember to pack repair kits and plenty of water.

Bike Rentals   For hourly or daily bike rentals, as well as maps and suggestions on local mountain biking, call **Bighorn Bike Adventures**. Their inventory includes mountain bikes, cruisers, tandems, and kids' bicycles. Bighorn also schedules guided bicycle adventures, including tours of Indian Canyons and celebrity neighbor-

hoods. Closed Wednesday. ~ 302 North Palm Canyon, Palm Springs; 760-325-3367. Another company, **Adventure Bike Tours**, also rents bicycles and offers guided tours. ~ Rancho Mirage; 760-328-0282. Based in Palm Desert, **Big Wheel Bike Tours** delivers a variety of bikes to area hotels and can arrange guided tours. ~ 760-779-1837; www.bwbtours.com.

Hiking

What distinguishes Palm Springs from other California tourist destinations is its proximity, for hiking enthusiasts, to both desert and mountain environments. The west side of the Coachella Valley is dominated by the tall, unscarred San Jacinto range, connected to the arid basin by a series of stream-cut canyons.

East, north, and south of Palm Springs are vast stretches of desert punctuated by mountains of varying heights. Many of these ranges have trail networks and parklands with their own singular attractions, suitable for hikers of every ability.

All distances listed for trails are one way unless otherwise noted.

PALM SPRINGS AREA The areas adjacent to Palm Springs offer numerous hiking adventures. Beginning within the city limits, the **Museum Trail** (1 mile) ascends the low mountain behind the Palm Springs Desert Museum. Markers along this nature trail describe the plants and other features of this terrain.

Several canyons, known collectively as the **Indian Canyons**, are accessible almost from within the Palm Springs city limits. The "Indians" include Tahquitz, Murray, Palm, Fern, and Andreas canyons, each noted for abundant native plant life, scenic waterways, and majestic fan palms. Deer, bighorn sheep, coyotes, and smaller mammals are frequent visitors. Most of this land is owned and managed by the Agua Caliente band of the Cahuilla Indians, with information and maps available at both the Tahquitz

A Hike to Remember

Near the Cottonwood Visitors Center in Joshua Tree National Park, one of the most memorable hikes is the strenuous **Lost Palms Oasis Trail** (3.75 miles), which winds through a series of canyons and streambeds to a remote grove of native palms surrounded by walls of rock. Lucky hikers sometimes see bighorn sheep browsing or drinking here.

Canyon Visitors Center and the Cahuilla Trading Post. Hours and access vary, depending on location and season. Some sites are accessible to individuals, while others can only be seen on ranger-led hikes. Admission. ~ 38520 South Palm Canyon Drive, Palm Springs; 760-325-3400, 800-790-3398; www.indian-canyons.com, www.tahquitz canyon.com.

In **Palm Canyon**, an easy-to-difficult, self-guided trail begins at the Cahuilla Trading Post and descends into the canyon and through the largest stand of fan palms in the world. This well-traveled trail winds back and forth across a perennial stream. You can hike distances of a half-mile to 13 miles. The hardiest adventurer may wish to explore the 3200-foot-high ridges that overlook the canyon. Other trails in the area include the moderate

Hike the San Jacinto Mountains

From Mountain Station at the top of the Palm Springs Aerial Tramway, there's an exhilarating six-mile hike along Mount San Jacinto Trail to the 10,804-foot summit. A shorter, two-and-a-half-mile trek leads through pine and fir to Round Valley.

If these don't interest you, there are a total of 54 miles of maintained trails to choose from atop Mt. San Jacinto. Remember to bring extra clothes, food, and water. To hike in the Mt. San Jacinto wilderness, you must have a permit. Self-issuing day permits are available at the ranger station, about a quarter-mile from Mountain Station, where the tram discharges passengers. Overnight permits may be arranged in advance by mail (send a self-addressed, stamped envelope to Mt. San Jacinto State Park, P.O. Box 308, Idyllwild, CA 92549). For weather updates, call 760-327-0222. For other information about hiking in the park, contact the ranger station in Idyllwild at 909-659-2607; www.sanjac.state park.org.

Palm Springs
Aerial Tramway

Fern Canyon Trail (2.5 miles) and **Victor Trail** (2.5 miles), as well as the strenuous **Maynard Mine Trail** (4 miles) that starts in Andreas Canyon.

For informative guided hikes through the Indian Canyons and elsewhere in the Palm Springs area, of varying degrees of difficulty, contact **Desert Safari** in Rancho Mirage (760-770-9191) or **Big Wheel Tours** in Palm Desert (760-779-1837).

For a splendid view of Palm Springs and the Coachella Valley, climb the **Shannon Trail** (3.5 miles), a steep hike that ascends 1522-foot Smoke Tree Mountain.

At the eastern end of the Living Desert Reserve sits **Eisenhower Mountain Trail** (3 miles). The path crosses

a wash and climbs up the mountain slope for sweeping vistas of the Coachella Valley.

Bear Creek Canyon Trail (2 miles), near La Quinta, also probes a desert valley. In the spring after rains, this lovely area is alive with golden poppies and a bubbling creek.

Another vantage point is reached via **Edom Hill Trail** (3 miles). In the center of the Coachella Valley, this 1610-foot promontory offers panoramic views of Mt. San Jacinto, Mt. San Gorgonio, and the Salton Sea.

In Mecca Hills, **Painted Canyon Trail** (3 miles) explores a beautifully sculpted canyon.

JOSHUA TREE NATIONAL PARK AREA Joshua Tree National Park, northeast of Palm Springs, is an area where High Desert meets the Low Desert, providing marvelous hikes through both of these distinctive environments. Hikers have dozens of well-marked trails to choose from, leading through boulder-strewn valleys, wildflower-dotted meadows, and rocky foothills. Destinations include old mines and homesteads, hidden springs, palm oases, and perennial tanks (the local term for ponds). You'll want to pick up trail maps and descriptions at one of the park's visitors centers.

Ryan Mountain Trail (1.5 miles) is a prime place to view both the Joshua trees and granite outcroppings for which the park is renowned. This difficult trail, which leads to the top of Mount Ryan (5470 feet), also offers views of several valleys.

Another overlook is reached along **Mastodon Peak Trail** (1.5 miles). Atop the 3371-foot promontory, the Hexie Mountains, Pinto Basin, and the Salton Sea extend before you.

Hidden Valley Trail (1-mile loop), beginning near Hidden Valley Campground, is a twisting loop through boulder-strewn desert to a legendary cattle rustler's hideout.

From Canyon Road, **Fortynine Palms Oasis Trail** (1.5 miles) is a moderate hike to a refreshing desert oasis.

Skull Rock Trail (.25 mile). is a highly recommended trek through some interesting boulder piles near Jumbo Rocks Campground.

Lost Horse Mine Trail (2 miles) takes you to an old gold mine. It's a moderately strenuous hike that should be avoided in hot weather—there is no shade or water en route.

A less taxing trip for anyone intent on exploring abandoned diggings is the **Desert Queen Mine Trail** (.2-mile overlook), located north of Geology Tour Road (a four-wheel drive vehicle is recommended on this route).

The **Cottonwood-to-Morton Mill Trail** (.5 mile) leads to the ruins of an abandoned gold-refining mill.

For the hearty hiker, **Boy Scout Trail** (8 miles) leaves from Indian Cove and traverses the western edge of Wonderland of Rocks.

Ideal for families, **Arch Rock Nature Trail** (.3-mile loop) in White Tank Campground wanders through intriguing rock formations while signs help interpret the geology of the region.

TRANSPORTATION

Car

Route 10, the San Bernardino Freeway, extends east from Los Angeles through the heart of the Inland Empire and Low Desert. Under normal conditions, it's about a two-hour drive (110 miles) from Los Angeles to Palm Springs.

About 12 miles northwest of Palm Springs, **Route 111** leaves Route 10 and curves southeast through Palm Springs (as Palm Canyon Drive) and through the Coachella Valley to Indio. Four miles farther east of the

Route 111 exit on Route 10, **Route 62** leads northeast to Joshua Tree National Park.

From San Diego, take **Routes 15** and **215** north to **Route 60**, then continue northeast to Route 10. Follow Route 10 east, exiting on Route 111 to Palm Springs. Allow about three hours for the 140-mile drive from San Diego to Palm Springs.

Air

Carriers serving **Palm Springs International Airport**, located about two miles from downtown, include Alaska/Horizon Airlines, America West, American Airlines, American Eagle, Continental, Delta, Northwest, Sky-West, Sun Country, United Express, and WestJet. ~ Palm Springs International Airport, 3400 East Tahquitz Canyon Way at North El Cielo Road, Palm Springs; 760-318-3800; www.palmspringsairport.com.

*Palm Springs
Air Museum*

Bus

Greyhound Bus Lines (800-231-2222; www.greyhound.
com) offers service in Palm Springs at 311 North Indian
Canyon Drive, 760-325-2053; and in Indio at 45-525
Oasis Street, 760-347-5888.

Train

Amtrak (800-872-7245; www.amtrak.com) has daily
service to Palm Springs (North Indian Canyon Drive and
Amado Road) and Palm Desert (Monterey Avenue and
San Gorgonio Way).

Car Rentals

Several agencies are located at the Palm Springs airport terminal: **Avis Rent A Car** (800-331-1212), **Budget Rent A Car** (800-527-0700), **Dollar Rent A Car** (800-800-4000), **Enterprise Rent A Car** (760-778-0054), **Hertz Rent A Car** (800-654-3131), and **National Car Rental** (800-227-7368).

If you're looking for a jeep, contact **Aztec Rent A Car**. ⁓ 477 South Palm Canyon Drive, Palm Springs; 760-325-2294; www.azteccarrentals.com.

Public Transit

Scheduled public buses operated by **SunLine Transit** carry passengers to destinations throughout the Coachella Valley. ⁓ 760-343-3456, 800-347-6828; www.sunline.org.

Taxi

The Palm Springs area has several taxi companies, including **Executive Taxi**. ⁓ 495 South Industrial Place, Palm Springs; 760-864-1500. **City Cab Palm Springs** is another option. ⁓ 3666 East Paseo Barbara, Palm Springs; 760-321-4470. City Cab also operates taxis in Rancho Mirage, Palm Desert, and Indio.

There are more than a dozen limousine services for those who want to go out for the evening or travel to the airport in style, among them **Red Carpet Limousine**. ⁓ 38471 Bel Air Drive; 760-325-4116. Another provider is **Palm Springs Limo Service and Public Shuttle**. ⁓ 255 North El Cielo Road; 760-320-0044. Airport shuttle service to and from Palm Desert is provided by **Valley Cabousine**. ⁓ 760-340-5845.

Jeep Tours

Backcountry jeep tours are a great way to explore the desert and learn about it natural and human history.

Desert Adventures Wilderness Jeep Tours offers guided two-to-four-hour trips bearing such names as Sunset-Nightwatch, Lost Legends of the Wild West, Indian Culture, and Mystery Canyon. The outfitter takes visitors as far afield as Joshua Tree National Park. ~ 67555 East Palm Canyon Drive, Cathedral City; 760-324-5337, 888-440-5337; www.red-jeep.com. Another company offering off-road tours is **Canyon Jeep Tours in Palm Springs**. ~ 15831 La Vida Drive; 760-320-4600. **Five Star Adventures** features a San Andreas Fault Jeep Tour with a naturalist guide. ~ 760-320-1500.

Think you can handle an ATV or a dune buggy? You can rent your own off-road vehicle in Palm Springs at **Offroad Rentals**. The company provides instruction as well as access to a privately owned desert dune area. ~ 59511 Route 111; 760-325-0376.

2.

Palm Springs

Take a desert landscape thatched with palm trees, add a 10,000-foot mountain to shade it from the sun, then place ancient mineral springs deep beneath the ground. Create a spot where the average annual daily temperature swings from a crisp 55 degrees to a toasty 85 degrees. What you have is a recipe for one of the few scenic Western locales where winter brings the best weather. A fashionable health spa, golf refuge, and celebrity playground, Palm Springs is the ultimate destination for sunning, swimming, and shopping.

Here, visitors can browse impressive museums, patronize fine restaurants, and sample diverse nightlife, including a campy variety stage show performed by gray-haired show biz

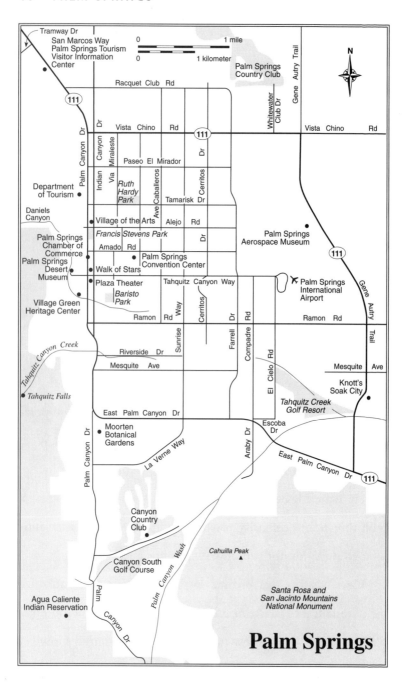

Palm Springs

veterans. In recent years, Palm Springs has become known for its unique art galleries and specialty stores. Many sell high-quality antiques, quirky consignment goods, and vintage furnishings from the 1950s and '60s. The city is widely recognized for its careful preservation of mid-20th-century modern homes and other buildings designed by such forward-thinking architects as Albert Frey, Lloyd Wright (son of Frank), and Richard Neutra.

Be advised that many attractions and businesses close or have limited hours during the hot summer months, so check in advance if visiting between June and October. On the plus side, bargain prices are often offered by those establishments that do remain open.

San Gorgonio Pass Wind Farm

As you drive through San Gorgonio Pass on Route 10 on your way to Palm Springs, you can't help but notice the thousands of white, propeller-driven turbines mounted on stilts above the ground that are spun by a near-constant flow of wind. One of the three largest wind farms in the world, spread over 70 square miles, this operation delivers electricity mainly to Southern California Edison. The utility gets about four percent of its power from wind turbines; California as a whole derives one percent of its electricity from such winds farms. Each of the privately owned turbines costs about $300,000 and can generate from 75 to 700 kilowatts. The downside? Many birds are killed by these machines—it's a true environmentalist dilemma.

San Gorgonio Pass is ideal for wind-power generation, since the air is funneled naturally between two very tall mountain ranges. As temperatures rise in the Coachella Valley, cool air is sucked in from the west. The average wind speed here is 15 to 20 miles per hour, which the industry considers perfect. Get close enough to them and you'll feel the exhilarating whoosh of air as the nearly silent windmills make use of nature's virtually inexhaustible energy. A tour of this forest of spinning propellers has been dubbed "the ultimate power trip."

Learn first-hand why San Gorgonio Pass was labeled one of the breeziest spots on Earth by NASA scientists, who helped design the wind farm. Several outfitters offer narrated tours by Jeep, bus, or dune buggy. Well-informed guides explain the history of wind power and where the generated electricity goes. Elegant in their simplicity, the towering windmills sigh and whir as they spin overhead. Fascinating and educational, each tour lasts from 90 minutes to two hours. Bring a jacket, wear a hat, and have your camera ready. Reservations required, though several scheduled tours are usually offered daily. Among local operators offering guided windmill tours are: **Best of the Best Tours** (760-320-1365, 877-449-9466; www.bestofthebesttours.com, e-mail pscjt@aol.com) and **Dunebuggy Tours** (760-322-7023; www.dunebuggytours.com).

SIGHTS

Several local agencies are available to direct you, divert you, and help you determine an itinerary for your Palm Springs visit. Information, maps, and friendly suggestions are available from the city's **Department of Tourism** at two in-town locations and on the Internet. Open daily. ~ 777 North Palm Canyon Drive and 2901 North Palm Canyon Drive; 760-327-2828, 760-778-8418, 800-347-7746; www.palm-springs.org, e-mail information@palm-springs.org. A business directory that includes dining, shopping, and lodging information can be obtained at the **Palm Springs Chamber of Commerce**. Closed weekends. ~ 190 West Amado Road; 760-325-1577, fax 760-325-8549; www.pschamber.org, e-mail pschamber@pschamber.org.

A must-see attraction is the **Palm Springs Desert Museum**, one of California's great regional art centers. Contained in a dynamic and contemporary structure

Tramway Oasis Gas Station

Text continued on page 54.

Uptown Heritage District

Because of its soaring heat and glaring sun, Palm Springs is not as conducive to walking as communities blessed with moderate climates. Nevertheless, comparatively mild November-through-April temperatures and a concentrated downtown core make the oldest part of the city an attractive place to explore on foot. Set out during morning or evening and take advantage of the flexible hours that many businesses maintain as a way to encourage shopping in the cooler parts of the day.

Start your stroll north of the tourist attractions that dominate the busy heart of the Heritage District (also called The Village), between Andreas and Baristo roads on Palm Canyon Drive. Kick off at **Koffi**, a retro-chic coffeehouse that embraces Palm Springs modernism without taking it too seriously. Enjoy your caffeine buzz and fresh pastry in a friendly atmosphere that affords equal opportunity to read the paper, check your e-mail, or ask locals what's going on. ~ 515 North Palm Canyon Drive; 760-416-2244.

Head north along this lively border zone between the history-laden Heritage and non-mainstream Uptown districts, an area marked by an intriguing assortment of art galleries, small hotels, funky bookstores, professionals' offices, ethnic restaurants, and that Palm Springs mainstay: the vintage clothing and used furniture retailers. Among the best is **Revivals Gallery**, a resale shop with an attitude. Here you may find everything from a Bette Davis ashtray collection to a Versace bedspread, from a 1950s martini shaker to a 1960s sofa with built-in fondue pit. Revivals is a nonprofit enterprise that donates its proceeds to local charities. Closed Tuesday. ~ 745 North Palm Canyon Drive; 760-318-1892.

Continue north and you'll encounter the **El Paseo Building**, one of several architecturally significant structures in this neighborhood. Built in 1926, this two-story complex is a good example of the Spanish Eclectic style that preceded modernism as a popular Palm Springs design. Although the façade has been altered, note the tile-covered gable roof and shaded window balconies. ~ 800 North Palm Canyon Drive, at the corner of Tamarisk Road.

Directly across Tamarisk Road is a handsome two-story 1936 mission revival building with Mediterranean and Spanish elements that were prominent hereabouts before World War II. ~ 766-798 Palm Canyon Drive.

A few doors down in a modern building is **Urban Yoga**, where visitors of any ability are welcome to drop in for a rejuvenating class. Actress-model Mariel Hemingway stretches here. ~ 750 North Palm Canyon Drive; 760-320-7702.

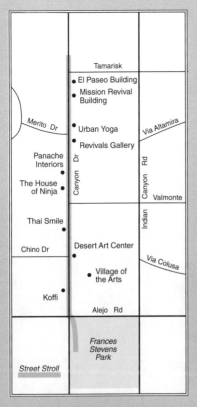

Tamarisk

- El Paseo Building
- Mission Revival Building
- Urban Yoga
- Revivals Gallery

Merito Dr

Via Altamira

Panache Interiors

Canyon Dr

Canyon Rd

The House of Ninja

Valmonte

Thai Smile

Indian Canyon

Chino Dr

Desert Art Center

Via Colusa

- Village of the Arts

Koffi

Alejo Rd

Frances Stevens Park

Street Stroll

---

sidered every detail when creating their Japanese restaurant. In addition to authentic Japanese entrées, there's an elaborate sushi bar serving fish flown in daily from around the world. ~ 707 North Palm Canyon Drive; 760-322-5565.

Keep going south to the middle of the next block if you're in the mood for what some locals insist is the city's best Thai food, served by the friendly staff at **Thai Smile**. A quick and delicious bargain is the lunch special. Beautifully decorated, the restaurant also serves dinner. ~ 651 North Canyon Drive; 760-320-5503.

Last stop is the **Desert Art Center**, a fine-art gallery showcasing works by talented local artists working in a variety of media. The gallery is in a renovated mission revival–style school, built in 1927 and dedicated by President Gerald Ford in 1974 as a cultural arts center. It includes the Palm Canyon Theater, where you might catch a play. Also adjacent is tree-shaded Frances Stevens Park. ~ 550 North Canyon Drive at Alejo Road; 760-323-7973.

You can head back to where you started by meandering along parts of Palm Canyon Drive you may have missed, or go a block east to Indian Canyon Drive, then turn north and proceed parallel to Palm Canyon passing another eclectic mix of shops and restaurants.

Cross Palm Canyon and continue south to **Panache Interiors**, which specializes in both antique and new home furnishings and accessories, with a particular emphasis on European origins. ~ 725 North Palm Canyon Drive; 760-416-9001.

A few doors down is **The House of Ninja**, whose owners painstakingly con-with a stone facade, the museum combines desert art and culture. There are exhibits of basketry by indigenous Cahuilla Indians and stark black-and-white photos of the American West. Set against the mountains in an exclusive section of downtown Palm Springs, the complex houses many works of contemporary art as well as galleries devoted to classic Western American, Mexican, pre-Columbian, and American Indian art. The most appealing places of all are the restful sculpture gardens, adorned with splashing fountains and native palms. There's also a

*Palm Springs
Desert
Museum*

café, gift shop, lecture hall, education center, and the 433-seat Annenberg Theater, where music, dance, and other performances are staged. In 2004, a natural sciences wing was replaced with a new art gallery. An interpretive nature trail behind the museum leads to the top of a low mountain that overlooks the city. Closed Monday. Admission, except Thursday from 4 p.m. to 8 p.m. ~ 101 Museum Drive; 760-325-7186, fax 760-327-5069; www.psmuseum.org, e-mail info@psmuseum.org.

A few blocks east of the museum is Palm Canyon Drive, site of the downtown **Palm Springs Walk of Stars**. In the style of Hollywood's Walk of Fame, gold stars embedded in the sidewalk memorialize such frequent celebrity visitors as Sophia Loren, Elvis Presley, Marilyn Monroe, and William Powell. You'll also see bronze statues of comedienne Lucille Ball and singer/businessman Sonny Bono, both of whom once figured prominently in the community. ~ Palm Canyon Drive, between Alejo Road and Tahquitz Canyon Way.

The earlier human story of Palm Springs unfolds within the historic buildings of the **Village Green Heritage Center**, a tiny park at the epicenter of downtown's

Village District. Closed
Monday and Tuesday,
and June to mid-October.
Admission. ~ 221 South
Palm Canyon Drive; 760-
323-8297, fax 760-320-
256; www.palmsprings.
com/history, e-mail palm
spgshistory@aol.com.

The best place to begin
is in the **Agua Caliente
Cultural Museum**, where
thoughtfully curated ex-
hibits illustrate the patrimony of the Agua Cal-
iente Indians, who settled
and still reside in the area.
In addition to the pho-
tographs, video, and artifacts on display, there is a full-
size Agua Caliente dwelling, small gift shop and information center. The museum's educational programs
include exhibitions and classes by contemporary Agua
Caliente artisans, writers, and musicians. Closed Monday and Tuesday, with shorter hours June through August. ~ 219 South Palm Canyon Drive; 760-323-0151,
fax 760-322-7724; www.accmuseum.org, e-mail accmu
seum@accmuseum.org.

Adjacent is **Ruddy's General Store Museum** (760-
327-2156). A re-creation of a 1930s-era general store,
this remarkable museum is literally lined with tins of
Chase & Sanborn coffee, boxes of Rinso Detergent, and
an entire wall of apothecary jars. One of the most complete collections of its kind, it showcases an inventory of

over 6000 items, most filled with their original contents. The store has penny gumball machines, nickel candy bars, and, yes, Prince Albert in a can. Closed Monday through Wednesday from October through June, and Monday through Friday from July through September. Admission.

Next door, in the **McCallum Adobe Museum** (760-323-8297), you'll see tools, fashions, children's toys, paintings, and books from the city's early years. Constructed in 1884 and '85 using local clay and sand, this is the town's oldest extant building, relocated from its original location. It displays a diverse array of items collected by the Palm Springs Historical Society, which includes vintage photos of Hollywood stars. A favorite is one of Groucho Marx without his trademark moustache. Closed Monday and Tuesday, and June to mid-October. Admission.

The mini-park's fourth museum is **Cornelia White's House** (760-323-8297). It was built in 1893 out of railroad ties as the home of a physician and later occupied by a pioneer woman, Miss White, and her sister. The house features antique furniture and such early-20th-century appurtenances as a wrought-iron wood stove and the community's first telephone. Closed Monday and Tuesday, and from May to mid-October. Admission.

At the south end of Palm Springs is one of the most luxuriant

The Unique Architectural History of Palm Springs

During the middle decades of the 20th century, the towering mountains and tawny sands surrounding this desert refuge inspired an elegantly informal aesthetic known as Palm Springs modernism. A combination of factors, including the willingness of wealthy clients to allow talented and progressive architects to experiment with entertainment-oriented vacation homes, led to the creation of unusual yet alluring structures of every size, shape, and function. Palm Springs modern is noted for its abundance of clean lines, glass or metal walls, flat roofs, sharp angles, simple landscaping, and the blurring of indoor and outdoor living spaces, often around sun-shading porches and shimmering swimming pools. Remarkably, much of this now-historic legacy still exists, allowing visitors to stay in hotels, dine in restaurants, and shop in distinctive buildings designed by such architects as Albert Frey, Lloyd Wright, Donald Wexler, William Cody, and Richard Neutra. Most classic Palm Springs modern homes and hotels are concentrated in the Tennis Club and Las Palmas neighborhoods, while civic and commercial structures are concentrated in the downtown Heritage district. Further information and a detailed map of Palm Springs modern addresses are available from the city's Department of Tourism or the Palm Springs modern Committee at either www.palm-springs.org or www.psmodcom.com.

and tranquil labyrinths you will ever explore. The **Moorten Botanical Garden** was established as a private arboretum in 1938 by a botanist and her husband and is now operated by the couple's son, Clark. The overgrown property displays over 3000 varieties of desert flora, along with glistening crystals, ancient fossils, and pioneer relics. Tours are self guided, with a helpful map provided upon admittance. Among the flourishing plants are prickly pears, ironwood trees, mesquites, agaves, boojums, succulents, and a desert's worth of cacti in what claims to be the world's first "cactarium" greenhouse. This is a charming refuge, inhabited by indigenous birds, lizards, and turtles, with a nursery where you can buy sun-loving plants for your own home. Next to a palm-shaded oasis and peaceful meditation alcove is The Cactus Castle, the Moorten's Mediterranean-style home. Closed Wednesday. Admission. ~ 1701 South Palm Canyon Drive, Palm Springs; 760-327-6555.

Drive beyond the urban edge of Palm Springs along South Palm Canyon Drive, past golf courses and residential neighborhoods, and you will soon encounter a large **kiosk** that provides gated entry onto tribal lands carefully managed by the Agua Caliente band of Cahuilla Indians. This, the Agua Caliente's ancestral homeland, is a wonderful place to hike, ride horses, or explore by car the foothills and canyons of the overshadowing San Jacinto range. Located just minutes from downtown Palm Springs, these little-disturbed natural treasures are a must-see attraction.

At the kiosk, a tribal employee will ask you where you are headed on the reservation and require a fee accordingly. Questions are answered and printed information (including maps) cheerfully dispensed. Most visitors are

Downtown Tours

For a close-up look at the city's celebrity homes and architecturally significant buildings, join a scheduled motorized or walking tour, or take a self-guided excursion by foot, car, or bicycle. Maps for self-guided tours are available for a fee from the Palm Springs Department of Tourism, each showing the exact location of more than 60 structures along with their renowned architects, builders, or occupants. During cooler months, a terrific way to see such sights is by bicycle, easily obtained from local hotels or rental agencies. Try **Big Horn Bike Adventures** (760-325-3367) for guided celebrity and architecture tours. For those who prefer a guided bus trip, **Palm Springs Tours** (877-656-2453; www.palm springsfuntrips.com) shows off the homes of Jack Benny, Elvis Presley, Goldie Hawn, and Kirk Douglas, among others. Similar tours are provided by **Palm Springs Celebrity Tours** (760-770-2700) and **Best of the Best Tours** (760-320-1365; www.bestof thebesttours.com). **P.S. Modern Tours** (760-318-6118; e-mail psmoderntours@aol.com) provides guided motorized and walking tours with an architectural theme.

going to one of several recreation areas maintained by the tribe for use by the general public. (Those wishing to explore Tahquitz Canyon, also owned and managed by the Agua Caliente, must proceed via Mesquite Drive to the Tahquitz Canyon Visitors Center; see below.)

An excellent orientation and starting point to this area is the **Cahuilla Trading Post**, situated two-and-a-half miles south of the entry kiosk at the terminus of Palm Canyon Drive. Perched on a ridge that affords a spectacular view into Palm Canyon, the trading post has hiking maps and its staff can answer any questions you may have before you descend into the canyon itself. Some maps available here detail more than a dozen nearby trails and clearly mark elevation contours. The Agua Caliente–owned facility also sells snacks, souvenirs, post cards, jewelry, baskets, pottery, weavings, CDs, videos, DVDs, books, and various craft items made by or relating to not only the Cahuilla people but many other American Indian tribes. There's a shaded picnic area in front of the building and restrooms around the side. Ranger-led interpretive tours from the trading post take approximately 90 minutes and are about a mile in length over an easy trail. Fees and schedules vary. You can park a horse trailer here if you plan a horse trip; call head for details. ~ 38520 South Palm Canyon Drive; 760-325-3400, 800-790-3398; www.indiancanyons.com.

Revealing a glimpse of what life was like here when the area was the private domain of American Indians, the **Indian Canyons** are a string of four noncontiguous gorges that plunge down the steep escarpment of the San Jacinto Mountains. (A fifth once-inhabited canyon, Chino, is now dominated by the Palm Springs Aerial Tramway.)

Visitors can spend the day hiking, horseback riding, and picnicking in these preserves, or one can simply drive to three of the canyons (the exception being Tahquitz) and admire them from viewing areas only steps away from their parking lots (mountain biking and rock climbing are not allowed in this area, for conservation reasons). Yet another option is to take a guided tour, which lasts about two hours. Providers of Indian Canyon bus tours include Palm Springs–based **Best of the Best Tours** (760-320-1365; www.bestofthebesttours.com); jeep tours are offered by **Canyon Jeep Tours** (760-320-4600), and equestrian tours can be arranged through **Smoke Tree Stables** (760-327-1372).

A rugged mountain glen, **Andreas Canyon** is about a mile from the entry kiosk, with a large parking area right next to Andreas Creek, which usually has water year-round. You'll also park here for hikes into neighboring Murray Canyon and to the old Maynard Mine; see below. Andreas contains some ancient Agua Caliente petrogylphs as well as mortar holes ground into bedrock slabs by members of the tribe using stone metates (pestles) to pound beans, corn, and acorns into flour. The tumbling stream has sharply cut the canyon walls while watering the estimated 150 indigenous plant species that grow along its course. The hundreds of fan palms here make this the second-largest palm oasis in North America, after Palm Canyon. A well-marked, one-mile nature trail loops along both sides of the creek, making a U-turn at a fenced piece of private land occupied by a number of stone huts. There are abundant scenic spots along tranquil Andreas

Creek for taking pictures, picnicking, birdwatching, or simply contemplating nature's beauty. A formal streamside picnic area, with restrooms, is near the parking lot. From that same picnic ground, a (marked) strenuous trail wends its way for two-and-a-half miles to the abandoned diggings of Maynard Mine, near the head of Murray Creek.

From the Andreas Canyon picnic ground, an eight-tenths-mile trail leads to the smaller but no less beautiful **Murray Canyon**, where palm trees are mixed with cottonwoods, willows, and sycamores among the pools and

The Prosperity of Local American Indians

For 3000 years or more, various bands of Cahuilla Indians were the only human residents of the Coachella Valley. These ingenious people adapted to the extreme conditions of their natural environment by shuttling seasonally between the desert basin (in winter) and pine-covered mountains (in summer). Their most permanent communities were in the spring-watered, palm-shaded canyons that served as passageways between valleys and ridgetops.

Members of the Agua Caliente band of the Cahuilla tribe have lived in what is now the Palm Springs area for at least 2000 years. They trapped fish and waterfowl in ancient Lake Cahuilla until about the time Columbus arrived in the New World. They used plants growing beside the lake to make houses, baskets, clothes, and other items. Here and elsewhere they grew corn, squash, beans, and other foods.

Virtually ignored by the Spanish and Mexican settlers who controlled California through 1846, the U.S. government acknowledged Agua Caliente land claims by establishing a large reservation—albeit in a checkerboard pattern, shared with a railroad company—on their behalf in 1876. Around that time, most members of the band shifted from a subsistence hunting and gathering lifestyle to one based on farming, ranching, and running small businesses.

cataracts of Murray Creek. Mule deer, bighorn sheep, and wild horses occasionally are seen roaming through this secluded chasm and, at night, coyotes, skunks, and bobcats make forays here. The endangered least Bell's vireo is among the unusual birds sometimes spied nesting amid the foliage. The tree-shaded main trail extends for a mile and a half along the stream and connects with other trails that lead eventually to Palm Canyon.

The biggest of the four canyons, yet hidden in the folds of ridges and foothills, **Palm Canyon** stretches for 14 miles and contains more than 3000 California fan palms (also known as Washington or desert fan palms). Some of these tall, frond-skirted trees are an estimated 250 years old and their trunks have been blackened over the decades by wildfires. This is, by far, the largest palm oasis on the continent and is home to a diverse array of plants and animals. An island of luxuriant greenery in a desert sea, Palm Canyon also displays exotic rock formations, American Indian artifacts, cascading waterfalls, and shimmering pools along spring-nourished Palm Canyon Creek. A graded, non-strenuous gravel path winds through much of this enclave and hikers are welcome to meditate, picnic, and take pictures here. The main Palm Canyon trail, as in other canyons, connects with smaller, more difficult, and less improved trails that wind for many miles through the area. A distinct advantage of taking a ranger-guided hike is the chance to learn about Palm Canyon's geology, flora, fauna, and human history.

About three miles north of Palm Canyon, the once litter-filled and graffiti-marred **Tahquitz** (pronounced *Tah-quits*) Canyon has been restored to a comparatively pristine natural state through the joint efforts of the Agua

Caliente band and the city of Palm Springs. On land that is part of the reservation and where an old Cahuilla village once stood, the canyon features a spectacular 60-foot seasonal waterfall, where parts of the 1938 movie *Lost Horizon* were filmed, with Tahquitz representing the mythical paradise of Shangri-La. Petroglyphs, irrigation

systems, mortars, and other Agua Caliente artifacts may be seen here. You'll also find an abundance of native flora and fauna, including palm trees, of course. This canyon is considered the ancient spiritual home of the powerful Cahuilla shaman, Tah-kwish, for whom the place is named. Ranger-led hiking tours that last about two and a half hours begin at the visitors center, which has exhibits, an observation deck, a snack bar, a gift shop, and a theater that screens a video about the canyon. Hours

Shake It Up

Owned by the Morongo Band of Mission Indians since 1999, **Hadley Fruit Orchards** is a friendly, old-fashioned roadside business founded in 1931 by Paul and Peggy Hadley, who opened

a fruit stand here in 1951. The family cultivated and sold fruit and nuts from trees on this property and others in the area, becoming renowned in the 1970s for originating the "trail mix" now widely prized by hikers. Besides fruit and nuts, Hadley sells honey, produce, jellies, snacks, souvenirs, gift items, nutritional supplements, and some rather unusual products, ranging from eucalyptus-chip candy to colon cleanser. The company grows its own dates on land many miles southeast of here and uses them to make some of the best date shakes around. In addition to retail sales, there's an online store that offers recipes and e-mail specials. Adjacent are the sprawling Cabazon Factory Outlet Stores and Morongo Casino complexes. What's in a date shake besides dates? Ice cream, milk, and nutmeg. ~ Cabazon exit off Route 10, 16 miles west of Palm Springs; www.hadleyfruitorchards.com.

and tour schedules vary seasonally; call for details. Hikers must be able to navigate about 100 steep steps. Admission. ~ 500 West Mesquite Drive, off South Palm Canyon Drive; 760-416-7044; www. tahquitzcanyon.com.

If hiking the Indian Canyons is a bit much, you can soar into the San Jacinto Mountains with mechanical assistance on the **Palm Springs Aerial Tramway**. Climbing at a teeth-clattering 50-degree angle and ascending from 2643 feet to 8516 feet above sea level, this mountain shuttle makes Disney's Space Mountain seem like a cakewalk. The world's largest rotating tramcars, offering 360-degree views, are just icing on the cake. You pass through five distinct ecological life zones, from desert to alpine. The tram runs about every half-hour from 10 a.m. to 9:45 p.m, with extended hours on weekends and holidays. While you're waiting, you may want to check out the gift shop, snack bar, or viewing area at the lower level. The perennial stream that flows directly underneath the lower station once supported an Agua Caliente Indian village that has long since disappeared. Admission. ~ One Tramway Road, off Route 111, Chino Canyon; 760-325-1391; www.pstram way.com, e-mail pstramway@pstramway.com.

The reward for those white knuckles and waves of vertigo is a view of the Coachella Valley from Joshua Tree to the Salton Sea. On a clear day you might not see forever, but you will spot a mountain peak near Las Vegas,

The Tramway Oasis Gas Station

One of the first buildings seen by visitors driving into Palm Springs from the west is a strikingly modern and audaciously sculptural structure at Route 111's intersection with Tramway Road. Constructed in 1963 as the Tramway Oasis Gas Station, it later was remodeled and served as an art gallery before being acquired by the City of Palm Springs and turned into its Official Visitors Information and Hotel Reservation Center. This one-of-a-kind building, with a soaring roofline, was designed by Albert Frey, a groundbreaking Swiss architect whose work dots the local landscape and who participated in the gas station's remodeling. Renowned for his prominent role in the singular style known as Palm Springs modern, Frey also designed hotels, homes, churches, and civic buildings during his long career in the area. A monument to car-dominated Southern California, the Tramway Oasis Gas Station is noted for its diamond shape, curving block walls, and steel cantilevered roof. The focus of a hard-fought preservation battle, this iconic building now proclaims to the world that Palm Springs is proud of its architectural heritage. It is, as one critic wrote, "a visual exclamation point." ~ 2901 North Palm Canyon Road; 760-778-8418; www.palm-springs.org.

175 miles away. **Mountain Station** offers the usual snack bar and souvenir shop amenities, plus a slightly upscale restaurant called Elevations (760-327-1590), which serves lunch, dinner, and mixed drinks. While waiting to return, you can browse a small natural history museum and watch a movie about the building of the tram, a remarkable feat of engineering. There are extensive trails at the top, including a three-quarter-mile nature loop. The nearby **ranger station**, which serves this section of Mount San Jacinto State Park and Wilderness Area, has information on longer hikes over more than 50 miles of maintained routes, including one to the 10,800-foot summit of Mount San Jacinto. From mid-November to

mid-April, snow permitting, the Nordic Ski Center (760-327-0222) is open for cross-country ski and snow-shoe equipment rentals.

Back in town, aviation buffs will find one of the largest collections of operable World War II combat aircraft at the **Palm Springs Air Museum**, enhanced by evocative photographs and vintage memorabilia. The volunteer docents, many of them World War II veterans, will guide you through the air-conditioned hangars where these items are stored. Upstairs are several computers with flight-simulation software you can try, along with recorded oral histories of pilots. On special occasions, some of the museum's 26 prop-driven planes take to the air for breathtaking displays. There's a gift shop, kids' program, restoration center, 60-seat theater, and aviation library. Summer hours may vary. Admission. ~ Palm Springs International Airport, 745 North Gene Autry Trail; 760-778-6262; www.palmspringsairmuseum.org, e-mail info@air-museum.org.

Palm Springs Air Museum

For family fun, **Knott's Soak City U.S.A. Waterpark** features 18 major waterslides and attractions, including the 800,000-gallon Rip Tide Reef wave pool. There's also a surfing zone and family-interactive water playhouse. Open daily mid-March through Labor Day, then weekends through October. Admission. ~ 1500 Gene Autry Trail; 760-327-0499; www.soakcityusa.com.

LODGING

What stands out about accommodation choices in Palm Springs is their amazing diversity. There truly seems to be something for everyone here, from the extremely posh to the budget basic, and from the intimate bed and breakfast to the all-inclusive resort. You can find places promoting themselves as gay-friendly, charmingly historic, clothing-optional, men or women-only, family or pet-oriented, retro-chic, and golf or tennis-conducive. There are a number of small, boutique hotels in the lush Tennis Club neighborhood, just west of downtown. Farther from the city center, many full-service resorts are secluded behind tall trees and privacy walls. The standards of hospitality are high here, and whatever option you choose is likely to reward you with a relaxing, pleasurable stay in this incomparable desert oasis.

Ingleside Inn
200 West Ramon Road
760-325-0046, 800-772-6655, fax 760-325-0710
www.inglesideinn.com, e-mail contact@inglesideinn.com
30 rooms
MODERATE TO ULTRA-DELUXE

Travelers interested in rubbing elbows with show-biz types should consider the elegant Ingleside Inn, a restored hacienda-style estate built around a restful courtyard.

Ingleside Inn

Garbo slept here, they say, as did Sinatra, Schwarzenegger, and Shields. And why not? The double rooms, villas, suites, and mini-suites are luxurious, charming, and laden with unusual antiques as well as modern amenities. Extras include fireplaces, whirlpool baths, and terraces, but everyone gets the same attentive service. There's a fine lounge and restaurant on the premises, and you can opt for an American plan that provides all your meals.

Ballantines Hotel

1420 North Indian Canyon Drive
760-320-1178, 800-485-2808, fax 760-320-5308
www.ballantineshotels.com, e-mail info@ballantineshotels.com
14 rooms
ULTRA-DELUXE

This retro-themed complex bills itself as the city's "coolest place to stay" and its accommodations surround a courtyard pool. The interior patio has a blue astroturf sun deck, and different theme rooms—such as the Marilyn

Monroe and the Jasper Johns—that contain 1950s-era furniture by Eames, Miller, and Bertoin. The suites and rooms are very spacious; most have dressing areas and some are equipped with kitchens. Adults preferred.

La Mancha Resort and Spa
444 North Avenida Caballeros
760-323-1773, 800-255-1773, fax 760-323-5928
www.la-mancha.com, e-mail reservations@la-mancha.com
59 rooms
DELUXE TO ULTRA-DELUXE

The private villas at La Mancha Resort and Spa are the last word in romantic escapism. Spanish–Moroccan architecture, high arched windows, and massive ceiling beams give the accommodations a castle-like ambience. All the villas have private courtyards; many have private pools. Spa, tennis, a gym, and in-room dining are among the other amenities.

Desert House
200 South Cahuilla Road
760-325-5281, 800-549-9230, fax 760-325-6736
www.deserthouseinn.com, e-mail info@deserthouseinn.com
6 rooms
MODERATE TO ULTRA-DELUXE

At a small, personalized hotel it's rare to find yourself in the hands of seasoned, professional hôteliers. But the Tennis Club neighborhood's Desert House is an exception. Before purchasing and remodeling this ranch-style inn, the current owners had long careers in the hospitality business. Their work is a labor of love and it shows. You'll find four studios with kitchenettes, and two rooms with refrigerators; five rooms sit poolside. Interiors are decorated in a Southwest motif with Dutch doors and plantation shutters. If you can muster the energy to leave the courtyard pool and sun deck, you'll find yourself within walking distance of restaurants, nightclubs, and museums.

Casa Cody Hotel
175 South Cahuilla Road
760-320-9346, 800-231-2639, fax 760-325-8610
www.casacody.com, e-mail casacody@aol.com
23 rooms
MODERATE TO ULTRA-DELUXE

Casa Cody Hotel, the second oldest hostelry in Palm Springs, bills itself as "a country bed-and-breakfast inn." It has an intimate, hideaway feel that recalls the early gentility of Palm Springs. Casa Cody's guest rooms, distributed in five hacienda-style buildings, have been re-

The Agua Caliente Tribe's Spa Resort Casino

The hot mineral springs that the Agua Caliente Indians discovered hundreds of years ago are today part of downtown's sprawling Spa Resort Casino, situated on one of the large sections of the city that is tribe owned. Bubbling from the ground at 106 degrees and containing 32 trace minerals, these soothing waters made Palm Springs famous. They have also made the Spa a major attraction, though the spring is now diverted into a network of pipes and holding tanks. On the resort's grounds are two Roman-style tubs, an outside swimming pool, and spa facilities that include inhalation rooms, dry saunas, and hot baths.

The entire hotel is lavishly appointed with desert-colored carpets and fashionably contemporary decor. Each of its 228 guest rooms were remodeled in 2003. A pictorial history of the Agua Caliente tribe adorns the lobby walls and American Indian crafts are sold in the gift shop. Several restaurants and bars are on the premises along with a large casino, one of two operated by the Agua Calientes, the area's largest single landowner. ~ Hotel and spa: 100 North Indian Canyon Drive; 760-325-1461, 800-854-1279, fax 760-325-3344; www.sparesortcasino.com, e-mail hotel@src mail.net. ULTRA-DELUXE. Casino: 401 East Amado Road; 760-883-1000.

furbished in a Southwest-chic decor. All but two have kitchens and some have fireplaces. A separate one-bedroom guesthouse and a 1910 two-bedroom adobe, where Charlie Chaplin once stayed, are also available. Breakfast is served poolside. Amenities include private entrances, fireplaces, patios, two pools, and lush gardens.

Villa Royale Inn
1620 Indian Trail
760-327-2314, 800-245-2314, fax 760-322-3794
www.villaroyale.com, e-mail info@villaroyale.com
31 rooms
DELUXE TO ULTRA-DELUXE

After decades of catering to the wealthy, Palm Springs inevitably possesses numerous luxury resorts. Unlike many, Villa Royale Inn displays its richness in an understated fashion. Each of the rooms in this Tuscanesque complex follows an individual theme, reflecting the art and culture of a different European region. Many have kitchens, fireplaces, and private patios. Covering more than three acres, the grounds are a series of interior courtyards framed by pillars and planted in bougainvillea. Amid brick footpaths and asymmetrical gardens are two swimming pools, jacuzzis, and a restaurant. The complimentary breakfast is cooked to order by the lovely on-site Europa Restaurant and served alfresco.

The Willows Historic Palm Springs Inn
412 West Tahquitz Canyon Way
760-320-0771, 800-966-9597, fax 760-320-0780
www.thewillowspalmsprings.com, e-mail innkeeper@thewillows
    palmsprings.com
8 rooms
Closed July and August
ULTRA-DELUXE

With only eight exquisitely furnished rooms, The Willows is an exclusive retreat into privilege and class.

Located in the historic Tennis Club section of Palm Springs, this handsomely restored 1924 Italianate-style villa features a frescoed ceiling in the dining room, a garden waterfall, fireplaces, stone floors, handmade tiles, antiques, clawfoot tubs, and pedestal sinks. The inn attracts a diverse clientele that has included Albert Einstein, Shirley Temple, Clark Gable, and Marion Davies. Complimentary gourmet breakfast and evening wine reception are included.

Le Parker Meridien Palm Springs

4200 East Palm Canyon Drive
760-770-5000, 800-210-3429, fax 760-324-2188
www.palmsprings.lemeridien.com
131 rooms, 12 villas
ULTRA-DELUXE

The city's only five-star hotel is Le Parker Meridien Palm Springs, formerly the Givenchy Resort, subject of a $27-million remodel in 2004. Guests pay up to $5000 a night for the privilege of staying in the posh hotel, which boasts such amenities as frozen pool towels, 24-hour valet parking, Wi-Fi internet access in every room, and

Share a Celebrity's Bed

McLean Company Rentals will rent you a home once owned by such luminaries as Elvis and Liberace, or you can choose from scores of other houses and condominiums. The company specializes in high-end, luxury properties; you can check the selection online. ~ 477 South Palm Canyon Drive, Suite 1; 760-322-2500, 800-777-4606, fax 760-323-7878; www.ps4rent.com, e-mail info@ ps4rent.com. Another provider of vacation condos and homes for rent, including a few previously owned by celebrities, is **Vacation Palm Springs**. ~ 1276 North Palm Canyon Drive, Suite 208; 760-778-7832, 800-590-3110; www.vacationpalmsprings.com.

European red-clay tennis courts. Personalized service is *Le Parker* paramount on the 13-acre property, previously owned by *Meridien* legendary Western singer Gene Autry and talk show host *Palm Springs* Merv Griffin. Now part of the Parker Group luxury hotel chain, Le Meridien has two upscale restaurants, Norma's and Mister Parker's. Guests are pampered at the hotel's spa, gym, and beauty salon, whimsically dubbed The Palm Springs Yacht Club. Oh yes, that $5000-a-night room is the resort's presidential suite, formerly Autry's residence.

Tortuga Del Sol
715 East San Lorenzo Road
760-416-3111, 888-541-3777
www.tortugadelsol.com, e-mail palmsprings@tortugadelsol.com
12 rooms
MODERATE TO ULTRA-DELUXE

Among the nearly 30 Palm Springs resorts and hotels serving a gay clientele, the Tortuga Del Sol offers one- and two-bedroom suites and studios, some with full kitchens or kitchenettes. Tastefully appointed, the dozen guest rooms boast brilliantly colored walls and furniture with Southwestern wood accents. The resort affords complete privacy and allows nude sunbathing. The grounds have a poolside misting system, hammocks, jacuzzi, swimming pool, and other amenities. Men only.

Harlow Club Hotel
175 East El Alameda
760-323-3977, 888-547-7881
www.theharlow.com, e-mail info@theharlow.com
15 rooms
DELUXE TO ULTRA-DELUXE

Catering exclusively to gay men, Harlow Club Hotel bills itself as "a civilized Eden." Surrounded by tropical gardens, it features Spanish-style 1930s-era bungalows. The guest rooms, designed in award-winning style, include fireplaces and private patios. There's also a gym, spa, and rooftop sundeck. Breakfast and lunch are included in the rate.

El Mirasol Villas
525 Warm Sands Drive
760-327-5913, 800-327-2985
www.elmirasol.com, e-mail elmirasolps@aol.com
15 rooms
MODERATE TO ULTRA-DELUXE

Debuting in 1975 as Palm Springs' original gay resort, El Mirasol Villas has secluded bungalows in a garden setting. This stylish resort, built by industrialist Howard Hughes in the 1940s, has suites and studios with custom furnishings, wet bars, kitchens, and poolside patios, two clothing-optional heated pools, a steam room, and a jacuzzi/spa with outdoor shower. A misting system provides relief from the heat. Complimentary breakfast, drinks, lunch, and a Saturday barbecue are served poolside.

The Hacienda

586 Warm Sands Drive
760-327-8111, 800-359-2007, fax 760-778-7890
www.thehacienda.com, e-mail info@thehacienda.com
10 rooms
ULTRA-DELUXE

Clothing-Optional Options

Guests bare it all at several Palm Springs hotels catering specifically to "naturists." Like other area resorts, these properties feature well-appointed rooms (some with kitchens), large swimming pools, jacuzzis, spa services, and complimentary breakfasts. The difference, of course, is that staff and guests are encouraged to go *au naturel*. Choices include the 92-room **Desert Shadows Inn**, which offers a fitness room, lighted tennis court, café, and other amenities. ~ 1533 Chaparral Road; 760-325-6410, 800-292-9298, fax 760-327-7500; www.desertshadows.com. MODERATE TO ULTRA-DELUXE. A smaller resort, with 17 rooms, is the **Terra Cotta Inn**, located on spacious, garden-like grounds on the northeast side of Palm Springs. Built as The Monkey Tree in 1960 by famed architect Albert Frey, it was once a getaway for Marilyn Monroe, Katharine Hepburn, and Spencer Tracy. ~ 2388 East Racquet Club Road; 760-322-6059, 800-786-6938, fax 760-322-4169; www.sunnyfun.com, e-mail info@sunnyfun.com. MODERATE TO DELUXE.

Spread across two verdant acres, The Hacienda is an upscale retreat featuring ten rooms and suites, some with fireplaces, private patios, and kitchenettes. Along with two pools and a jacuzzi, there are manicured gardens and grassy areas at this refined gay-oriented getaway. Breakfast and lunch are served poolside or in your room.

Terrazzo

1600 East Palm Canyon Drive
760-778-5883, 866-837-7996, fax 760-416-2200
www.terrazzo-ps.com, e-mail info@terrazzo-ps.com
12 rooms
DELUXE TO ULTRA-DELUXE

Clothing-optional Terrazzo offers comfortable, air-conditioned rooms decorated in a Southwestern style. All units feature French doors overlooking a swimming pool and garden, as well as microwaves and refrigerators. There's a fully equipped gym on site and concierge service. Enjoy an expanded continental breakfast in the morning, delivered in bed if you wish. A catered gourmet lunch is included as well as complimentary snacks and drinks. Men only.

Chestnutz

641 San Lorenzo Road
760-325-5269, 800-621-6973, fax 760-320-9535
www.chestnutz.com, e-mail chestnutzps@aol.com
12 rooms
MODERATE TO ULTRA-DELUXE

Chestnutz, a luxury resort for men, serves a complimentary full breakfast and evening wine and hors d'oeuvres to its guests. The 12 rooms are individually decorated, with both queen- and king-sized beds available. The king suites feature private patios and full kitchens. There are some nice touches here such as welcome baskets, nightly turndown service, and free local phone calls.

A misting system over the pool and jacuzzi keep things cool, as does the clothing-optional rule.

Casitas Laquita
450 East Palm Canyon Drive
760-416-9999, fax 760-416-5415
www.casitaslaquita.com, e-mail caslaquita@aol.com
13 rooms
MODERATE TO DELUXE

An exclusive resort for women, the "very lesbian-friendly" Casitas Laquita occupies more than an acre of lush, flower-scented grounds with breathtaking mountain views. In-room continental breakfast is provided and massages are available on request. All of the Spanish Mission–style casitas have full kitchens, data ports, and are non-smoking; some have fireplaces and private outdoor dining areas. Furnishings are handcrafted and accented with carefully selected American Indian art objects.

Del Marcos Hotel
225 West Baristo Road
800-676-1214, fax 760-325-6909
www.delmarcoshotel.com, e-mail info@demarcos.com
16 rooms
DELUXE

Korakia
Pensione

Designed in 1947 by renowned modernist architect William Cody, this distinctive inn is centrally located a block east of Palm Canyon Drive in the Tennis Club district. Some rooms include kitchens, private patios, and balconies. Most are poolside. All guests have free use of vintage bicycles, which are a fun way to check out the nearby movie-star homes. Continental breakfasts and beverages are complimentary. Enjoy mid-20th century decor and music throughout this brilliantly restored property. Also, the Del Marcos has a furnished, Alexander-designed Palm Springs modern home for rent in the Las Palmas neighborhood.

Korakia Pensione
257 South Patencio Road
760-864-6411, fax 760-864-4147

www.korakia.com
29 rooms
DELUXE TO ULTRA-DELUXE

Built by Scottish artist and bon vivant Gordon Coutts, this Moroccan villa has hosted luminaries from the arts, politics, and show business since its construction in 1924. British Prime Minister Winston Churchill reportedly painted in its art studio. Filled with antiques, handcrafted furniture, Oriental rugs, canopied beds, and all manner of objects d'art, the Korakia is a bed and breakfast in the grand manner. Guests are housed in villas, bungalows, and guesthouses amid one-and-a-half acres of fruit orchards and gardens. Complimentary amenities include a full breakfast (served in-room if desired), kitchenettes, fireplaces, massage tents, outdoor movies, and a Moroccan tea service at sundown. The pampered ambience here is of an opulent North African oasis. Gay-friendly but not exclusive.

Space-Age Chic

For the ultimate Palm Springs modern experience, the 18-room **Orbit In** delivers the best of old and new. The owners operate two restored 1950s' motels—the Oasis is the main location, the Hideaway is just down the street—that have been restored to their original sleek-lined beauty. Themed rooms boast classic furniture and period artwork (including framed album covers) that transport occupants straight back to the Eisenhower era. Or is it "The Jetsons"? Cruiser bikes, afternoon cocktails, snacks, videos, board games, in-room martini shakers, continental breakfast, and data ports are complimentary. Other amenities include saltwater pools, cooling misters, a large jacuzzi, and boomerang-shaped outdoor bar. Some rooms have kitchenettes and all have refrigerators. The Orbit In is on a quiet side street yet close to the action of downtown Palm Springs. ~ 562 West Arenas Road; 760-323-3585, 877-996-7248, fax 760-323-3599; www.orbitin.com, e-mail mail@orbitin.com. DELUXE TO ULTRA-DELUXE.

DINING

Las Casuelas Terraza
222 South Palm Canyon Drive
760-325-2794, fax 760-778-6744
www.lascasuelasterraza.com
MODERATE TO DELUXE

A spacious hacienda with murals, fountains, and in-laid tile, Las Casuelas Terraza is a classic, festive Mexican dining room. Pass through the arched doorway and you'll discover hanging plants and wrought-iron decorations throughout. The outdoor patio features a *palapa* bar, a stage, and a dancing area. A step above other Mexican restaurants, the establishment serves *pollo asado*

Remembering Sonny Bono

For most of us, Sonny Bono is best known as half of the pop music duo Sonny and Cher, which rocketed to fame with the 1965 hit, "I Got You Babe." In Palm Springs, the singer gained local prominence during the late 1980s as the restaurateur who, frustrated with government red tape, ran for mayor and won. (During the campaign, the moderate Republican conceded that he had never voted before casting a ballot for himself, at age 53.) After his four-year term ended in 1992, Bono went on to become the area's Congressman and was flourishing in that capacity when he was killed in a freak skiing accident in early 1998. His widow, Mary, succeeded him in office. Sonny Bono, a resident of Palm Springs since his divorce from Cher in the 1970s, is often credited with bringing a new wave of Hollywood interest to the city by helping to found the Palm Springs International Film Festival. His concurrent clean-up campaign sidelined a rowdy downtown Spring Break tradition among college students that had kept more affluent would-be visitors away from town.

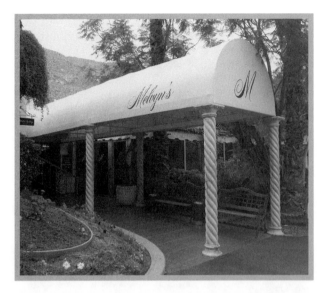

(marinated chicken), *pescado greco* (fish filet in garlic and wine), and *camarones florencio* (shrimp in salsa), as well as the standard south-of-the-border entrées.

Melvyn's
200 West Ramon Road, in the Ingleside Inn
760-325-2323
www.inglesideinn.com, e-mail contact@inglesideinn.com
Sunday brunch
DELUXE TO ULTRA-DELUXE

Melvyn's is one of those famous establishments with as many awards and celebrity glossies on the wall as items on the menu. Among the toniest addresses in town, it's a classic Continental restaurant complete with mirrors, crystal chandeliers, and wooden upholstered chairs. Celebrities have frequented the place for years. Its inventory of entrées includes Maryland crab cakes, grilled fish, and châteaubriand. There's a time-warp swinging jazz jam session in the adjacent bar on late Sunday afternoon.

Le Vallauris

385 West Tahquitz Canyon Way
760-325-5059
www.levallauris.com, e-mail vallauris@aol.com
dinner only
ULTRA-DELUXE

Le Vallauris is a bastion of upscale French cuisine and decor on a quiet side street near downtown. A piano bar sets the tone in this converted private residence for such satisfyingly rich dishes as duck foie gras and roasted rack of lamb. The soufflés are incredible and the service impeccable. A garden of ficus trees and blooming cyclamen warm this attractive two-room restaurant.

Rock Garden Café

777 South Palm Canyon Drive
760-327-8840
MODERATE TO DELUXE

Conveniently located on the way to the Indian Canyons, the tree-shaded Rock Garden Café's bill of fare runs from breakfast omelettes to lunch-time burgers, along with dinner entrées that include macadamia-crusted halibut and chicken fajitas. The food here is fine

Plum Crazy

An exceptionally attractive venue offering a choice of indoor or alfresco dining, **Plum** features an eclectic but refreshingly cosmopolitan menu that embraces everything from eggs Benedict to hearty Spanish *tapas* and all-American hamburgers. The emphasis is on fresh ingredients, imaginatively prepared. An enormous video screen dominates the bar, enclosed by a fanciful frame that clearly (and whimsically) reflects the establishment's gay-friendly disposition. Weekend brunch. ~ 241 East Tahquitz Canyon Way; 760-322-5280, fax 760-322-6179; www.plumfun.com. MODERATE TO DELUXE.

if not spectacular, but the outdoor deck above a lovely fountain-accented rock garden is one of the more inviting alfresco dining options in town.

Jensen's Deli
102 South Sunrise Way
760-325-8282
MODERATE

For scrumptious deli and specialty sandwiches, as well as upscale groceries and fresh baked goods, try Jensen's, a local grocery and deli chain with outlets in La Quinta and Palm Desert as well as Palm Springs. You can choose from among well-prepared hot or cold sandwiches named after such celebrated past residents as Walter Annenberg, Gene Autry, and Frank Sinatra.

Rainbow Cactus Café
212 South Indian Canyon Drive
760-325-3868
www.rainbowcactus.com
Sunday brunch
MODERATE

The Rainbow Cactus Café has a largely gay clientele and keeps it loyal with good home cooking: chicken and dumplings, liver and onions, and New York steak. The lunch line up consists of soups, salads, and sandwiches. At night, a piano bar swings into action.

Kaiser Grille
205 South Palm Canyon
760-323-1003
MODERATE TO DELUXE.

Known for its top-flight prime rib, the Grille also serves fresh fish, pasta, chops, steaks, and salads. There are also twilight specials and a bar menu. The food is excellent and you can sit in the stylishly contemporary dining room, on the people-watching deck out front, or along the roomy bar that connects the two. The same owners also operate two other deservedly popular restaurants across the street, the Chop House (serving steaks, chops, and fish, with a 3000-bottle wine cellar) and, right upstairs, The Deck (with a focus on Pacific Rim flavors with a Caribbean flair, served on a patio that is one of the best sunset-watching posts in town).

Spencer's At The Mountain
701 West Baristo Road, at the Palm
Springs Tennis Club Resort
760-327-3446
Sunday brunch
DELUXE TO ULTRA-DELUXE

Choose between a smartly elegant dining room and a tree-shaded, mist-cooled outdoor patio at Spencer's, a provider of sublime California cuisine with French and Pacific Rim influences. Entrées include veal, lamb, seafood, pastas, steak, and vegetarian items along with soups, salads, and appetizers. A typical dinner might start with kung pao calamari and advance through chilled gazpacho with Maine lobster before settling down to Dijon-coated New Zealand rack of lamb with fresh vegetables. Save room for the sinful pistachio créme brulée. Spencer's is equally suited to a casual after-golf lunch as it is for a more formal, special-occasion dinner. Free valet parking and occasional live piano.

Tyler's
149 South Indian Canyon Drive
760-325-2990
lunch only
MODERATE

The best testimonial to the quality of burgers, hot dogs, fries, shakes, and floats here is that locals are willing to stand in line for them, sometimes for a half-hour or more. Make sure you get your name on the list when you arrive, then grab one of the magazines or newspapers in the waiting area. The decor, service, and piped-in rock music are '50s basic, but for good ol' American comfort food Tyler's has few peers.

Peabody's Cafe, Bar, and Karaoke
134 South Palm Canyon Drive
760-322-1877
MODERATE TO DELUXE

The Heritage district of downtown has surprisingly few breakfast places, but Peabody's is a worthy exception. The menu and food are pretty standard, but portions are generous and you can dine under a sidewalk umbrella while watching the world go by. In addition, breakfast is available until 3:30 p.m. Since the Plaza Theater is right next door, this also is a good place for an early or late meal if you're attending the Palm Springs Follies. Local bands perform and the karaoke machine is cranked up on weekend nights.

Sherman's Deli and Bakery
401 East Tahquitz Canyon Way
760-325-1199
MODERATE TO DELUXE

A classic New York deli transported to the California desert, Sherman's will satisfy your craving for latkas, gefilte fish, pastrami, lox, knockwurst, and bagels. Come hungry, though, as portions are huge and a full sandwich is often enough for two people. And remember, the pastries and other baked goods are to die for. The dinner menu includes steak, whitefish, and other hearty entrées. There's a pleasant alfresco dining area, opposite the Spa Resort Casino, and a large indoor dining room, or phone ahead for takeout.

St. James At The Vineyard
265 South Palm Canyon Drive
760-320-8041
dinner only
DELUXE TO ULTRA-DELUXE

Surely one of downtown's most enchanting dining rooms and bars belongs to this international-themed restaurant, which beckons with subdued lighting, fine Asian sculpture, and a large collection of ethnic masks. A compelling and exotic fusion of Pacific Rim and California influences, dishes include beef, lamb, seafood, and pasta. Spicy curries and vegetarian gourmet entrées are specialties. A pleasing outdoor dining area overlooks the shopping arcade known as The Vineyard. There is often live music in the bar.

SHOPPING

Palm Canyon Drive, the Main Street of Palm Springs, contains the city's greatest concentration of specialty shops, although a significant number of distinctive retailers also line Indian Canyon Drive, which runs parallel a block to the east. There are almost as many signature stores as palm trees along these busy boulevards, particularly in the part of the Heritage district, between Amado Road and Baristo Road, known as **The Village**. Among the charming arcades and mini-malls here are The Vineyard (245 South Palm Canyon Drive), La Plaza (South Palm Canyon at La Plaza), The Promenade (123 North Palm Canyon Drive), Mercado Plaza (155 North Palm Canyon Drive), and The Cornerstone (301 North Palm Canyon Drive). While shopping, you'll find plenty of places to eat a meal, quaff a drink, or grab a snack. ~ www.palmcanyondrive.org.

R & R Menswear stocks contemporary, stylish clothing for the guy on the go. Beach wear, sports jackets, active wear, and club-geared garb can all be found here at moderate prices. ~ 333 North Palm Canyon Drive; 760-320-3007. Fashionable and high-quality shirts, trousers, and footwear for men are cheerfully dispensed at **Gerry**

Maloof Mens' Shop and Shoes. ~ 186 South Palm Canyon Drive; 760-325-2586.

For all things aloe, visit **Palm Springs Aloe People**. This unusual store carries an extensive line of skin moisturizers, tanning products, body scrubs, masks, and bath and shower gels. ~ 243 South Indian Canyon Drive; 760-323-0790. For novelty gifts, clever greeting cards, and fun gags, try **Paper Lilli**. ~ 114 North Palm Canyon Drive; 760-327-3373.

In the heart of The Village, **Adagio Galleries** exhibits an impressive collection of Latin American and Southwestern art. The inventory includes oil paintings, pastels, and bronze as well as sculptures and ceramics. Among prominent New Mexico painters represented are R.C. Gorman and John Farnsworth. Closed Tuesday and in August. ~ 193 South Palm Canyon Drive; 760-320-2230; www.adagiogalleries.com.

In fact, growing number of art galleries are being added to the shopping mix. Most are found along the Palm Canyon Drive corridor in the Heritage and Uptown districts, between Racquet Club Road to the north and

PICTURE-PERFECT
Shopping for New-to-You Items

1. **Revivals,** *p. 95*
2. **Celebrity Seconds,** *p. 95*
3. **Resale Therapy,** *p. 95*
4. **Vintage Oasis,** *p. 95*

Ramon Road at the south. While decorative and functional art prevails, many galleries also focus on abstract and post-modern fine art as well. Among the more interesting venues are **Austerer Crider Gallery** (448 North Palm Canyon Drive; 760-320-6955), exhibiting contemporary American artists working in a variety of media along with works on paper by the Masters; **The Carlan Gallery** (1556 North Palm Canyon Drive; 760-322-8002), specializing in continental antiques and art; **Firethorn Gallery** (406 North Palm Canyon Drive; 760-320-8684), owned by pastelist Clark Mitchell, who in addition to his own work shows paintings by Randall Sexton, Peggi Kroll-Roberts and others; **Heusso Gallery** (189 South Palm Canyon Drive; 760-322-8957), featuring whimsical art objects, original paintings, original edition prints, pottery, sculpture, glass, and French dolls; **Las Palmas Gallery** (861 North Palm Canyon Drive; 760-323-6983), focusing on fine art and vintage prints; and **The Palm Springs Gallery** (245 South Palm Canyon Drive; 760-320-1189), offering limited edition and original paintings by Thomas Kinkade, Cao Young, and Peter

Takin' It to the Street

A couple of enduring Palm Springs traditions draw thousands away from their air-conditioning on specific weekday evenings for a chance to buy and sell, see and be seen.

The busiest of the pair is **VillageFest**, a weekly twilight street fair on blocked-off Palm Canyon Drive. This open-air bazaar features food booths, live music, children's activities, booksellers, community information tables, political activists, massage practitioners, and scores of artists and artisans. There's even a certified farmers' market where you can stock up on fresh fruit, nuts, baked goods, and veggies. Many boutiques and specialty shops lining the street stay open late and move their sale merchandise onto the sidewalk for easy viewing. VillageFest is held throughout the year, from 6 p.m. to 10 p.m. from October through May, and from 7 p.m. to 10 p.m. June through September. ~ Village District, Palm Canyon Drive between Amado and Baristo roads; 760-320-3781.

Palm Springs' Uptown art and retail district is the focal point for **First Friday**, a festive event in which many merchants stay open until 9 p.m. and the scene is enlivened with food, entertainment, book-signings, and gallery exhibition openings. Held the first Friday of each month, this is a perfect time to get acquainted with the area's distinctive array of specialty restaurants, clothing boutiques, resale stores, antique shops, and galleries. ~ Uptown district, North Palm Canyon Drive between Amado Road and Tachevah Drive; 760-325-8979.

and Harrison Ellenshaw, with an emphasis on rom cized landscapes and figurative imagery.

Shopping for vintage or retro-chic clothing, fu housewares, and accessories has been elevated to fine art—and great fun—in Palm Springs as retailers have opened an eclectic mix of places to browse, buy, donate, and sell. Many of these outlets are found among the lower-rent addresses of North Palm Canyon and North Indian Canyon drives, but they also pop up in smaller shopping centers around town. Favorites include **Revivals** (611 South Palm Canyon Drive; 760-318-6491), a nonprofit entity that specializes in quality resale presented in an inviting atmosphere; **Celebrity Seconds** (333 North Palm Canyon Drive; 760-416-2072), with fine apparel and accessories, some worn by Ginger Rogers and other stars; **Vintage Oasis** (373 South Palm Canyon Drive, Studio A; 760-778-6224), where the emphasis is on mid-20th-century modern furnishings, clothes, and knick-knacks; and **Angel View Prestige Boutiques** (462 Indian Canyon Drive and 886 North Palm Canyon Drive; 760-322-2440), offering two stores stocked with a particularly amazing collection of women's clothing.

In an industrial area, east of downtown, you'll find three worthy destinations for used clothes and merchandise. **Estate Sale Company** occupies an entire block, featuring accessories, furnishings, pottery, and porcelains. ~ 4185 East Palm Canyon Drive; 760-321-7628. **Resale Therapy** features mainly women's clothes, from gold lamé stretch pants to feather boas—rumor has it that Tammy Faye Bakker shops here. ~ 4109 East Palm Canyon Drive; 760-321-6556. **Arrowhead Eclectics** stocks a particularly quirky melange of furnishings and antiques, including cowboy clothes and antiquarian books. ~ 2600 Cherokee Way; 760-324-4443.

A city where pampering is a major industry, Palm Springs has more than a dozen beauty salons and spas, most of them offering a variety of packages and custom services. Full-service providers include **Miko's Day Spa**, in the Hyatt Regency Suites Resort, which showcases massage, cellulite reduction, facials, waxing, microdermabrasion, and other treatments rendered by a staff of skin, nail, and body-care professionals. Amenities include several saunas and an outdoor jacuzzi pool. ~ Hyatt Regency Suites, 285 North Palm Canyon Drive; 760-320-6884, 877-329-7724; www.mikosdayspa.com. Another recommended destination for an indulgent day of beauty is the **Le Parker Meridien Palm Springs Spa**, located within one of the city's fanciest hotels. Besides the usual body, hair, face, and feet treatments, special treatments here include *lomi-lomi*, hot stone, and shiatsu massages as well as lymph drainage, reflexology, scrubs, three-treatment wraps, facials, and *watsu*. ~ 4200 East Palm Canyon Drive; 760-321-4606; www.parkermeridien. com. **Rosanna's Salon and Day Spa** provides a wide range of body, skin, hair, and nail treatments as well as massages and wraps. A speciality is its Dead Sea treatment, a cleansing skin treatment and massage that exfoliates and softens skin using mineral water and mud from the Dead Sea, along with moisture sage massage lotion. ~ 353 South Palm Canyon Drive; 760-325-4800; www. rosannas.com.

NIGHTLIFE

The Village Pub, a favorite haunt of Palm Springs locals as well as tourists, has live entertainment every afternoon and evening. The outdoor decks are inviting, or check out the upstairs, where there are pool tables, couches, 17 TVs tuned to sports, and patrons munching pub food or smoking premium cigars from the humidor. ~ 266 South Palm Canyon Drive; 760-323-3265; www.palmsprings villagepub.com.

You'll generally find a youngish crowd at the popular **Atlas Night Club**, in the heart of downtown, which has live bands or a deejay most every night. There's a great dance floor, full bar, and restaurant as well as a sidewalk seating area when you're ready to take a break. ~ 210 South Palm Canyon Drive; 760-325-8839.

The friendly atmosphere of **Street Bar Named Desire** explains why it's so popular among both locals and tourists. Although the clientele is primarily gay men, women and straight men also receive a hearty welcome. If you happen to be here on the right day at the right time, you might catch a drag show or a diva captivating the crowd. Otherwise, take a seat inside or on the outdoor patio, have a drink, and relax. ~ 224 East Arenas Road; 760-320-1266.

Over at the Wyndham Palm Springs Hotel, **The Lobby Bar** is a pleasant spot for a quiet drink for visitors of any age or persuasion. ~ 888 East Tahquitz Way; 760-322-6000.

For an authentic Polynesian vibe, don't miss the **Reef Tiki Bar** at the Caliente Tropic Resort. You'll find live music weekend nights and a jam session late Sunday afternoons. ~ 411 East Palm Canyon Drive; 760-327-1391.

Located in the Villa Resort, the **Dates Bar** features live music and comedy acts on Friday and Saturday nights.

The rest of the week, it's a great place for a quiet drink. ~ 67-670 Carey Road; 760-328-7211.

Badlands, a mellow neighborhood bar catering to a gay and lesbian clientele, is a good first stop for advice on the best local hot spots. ~ 200 South Indian Canyon Drive; 760-778-4326.

Heaven is a popular club where disco, drag, and karaoke are all in the mix. It's a party atmosphere, particularly on weekends. ~ 611 South Palm Canyon Drive; 760-416-0950.

Palm Springs has its share of friendly old-world pubs, offering drinks and food as well as occasional entertainment and open mikes. Try the **Hair of the Dog English Pub,** where there's live music, dancing and a Sunday barbecue. A friendly place with lots of character, you'll find electronic darts, pool tables, and a large outdoor patio for

The Fabulous Palm Springs Follies

Experience music, dance, song, and comedy of the 1930s and '40s at the historic Plaza Theater in downtown Palm Springs. In addition to hilarious variety acts and internationally known guest stars, the **Palm Springs Follies** are known for their legendary line of chorus "girls," none of whom are younger than 58—and include a fair number who crossed that threshold decades ago. Be prepared for corny vaudeville shtick and outrageous humor as well as burlesque, ventriloquism, and some sensational vocals by the likes of Kaye Ballard, Buddy Greco, and The Four Aces. Before the real fun begins, check out The **Palm Springs Hollywood Museum** on the premises, which further commemorates the golden age of American variety theater. The three-hour show, which changes regularly, runs from November through May, with matinees as well as evening performances. Admission. ~ 128 South Palm Canyon Drive; 760-327-0225; www.psfollies.com.

dining and drinking. ~ 238 North Palm Canyon Drive; 760-323-9890.

The **Annenberg Theater** at the Palm Springs Desert Museum is the hot ticket for big-name music, revues, jazz, opera, dance, Broadway, and comedy. The performance season runs from November through April with something scheduled virtually every week. Some events offer cocktails and/or dinner. Admission. ~ 101 Museum Drive; 760-325-4490; www.psmuseum.org.

Casino Morongo is an enormous, glitzy complex 16 miles west of Palm Springs. It includes a modern gaming hall, several restaurants, a concert auditorium, a state-of-the-art spa, and a 23-story hotel. An estimated $250 million was spent on expansions in 2004 by the tiny Morongo band of Mission Indians, underscoring the tribe's long-term faith in the gambling and hospitality businesses. This is, after all, the tribe whose policy-challenging lawsuits resulted in the landmark 1986 U.S. Supreme Court decision that opened the floodgates for tribal gaming throughout the country. Casino Morongo boasts hundreds of video and reel slot machines, both video and table power, blackjack and craps, with expanded Vegas-style gambling expected in the years ahead.

Tired of flash and glitter? The cozy, modest **Cahuilla Creek Casino** is in a remote area about an hour south of

For Nightowls

As the name implies, **The Blue Guitar** focuses mainly on jazz and blues, with live bands on weekends. It's an attractive club close to all the Village action. Sit on the open-air balcony for gorgeous views of the San Jacinto Mountains. ~ 120 South Palm Canyon Drive; 760-327-1549; www.blueguitar palmsprings.com.

Palm Springs, near Anza-Borrego Desert State Park and the tiny town of Anza. Operated by the 240-member Cahuilla band of Mission Indians, this unpretentious outpost features over 200 slot machines and about a dozen gaming tables where you can play blackjack and poker. Entertainment includes occasional concerts, live bands, and karaoke. A cocktail lounge and restaurant complete the package. ~ 52702 Route 371, Anza; 909-763-1200.

3.

Palm Springs Vicinity

outheast of Palm Springs, the Coachella Valley broadens into a flat, sandy plain that more than doubled in population (to more than 250,000 residents) during the final two decades of the 20th century. This is no longer simply a place where people retire, live part-time, or flock to as snowbirds—they actually live and work here, too. Bisected by busy Route 10, which flows through the Coachella Valley on its way from Arizona to the Pacific, most of the land from immediately west of the freeway to the foothills of the Santa Rosa and San Jacinto Mountains is now urbanized. East of Route 10 new housing developments are springing up, although there are irrigated farmlands and tracts of undisturbed desert as well.

The "main street" of the principal desert resort towns is Route 111, the state highway that threads its way from the wind farms outside Palm Springs through stop-and-go commercial strips and residential areas all the way to Indio, near where the valley is flooded permanently by the Salton Sea. For part of this 30-mile, west-to-east journey, Route 111 takes the name Palm Canyon Drive and in some areas both appellations are used.

Along Route 111 lies a contiguous series of cities—some of them extraordinarily wealthy—that

now compete aggressively with Palm Springs for the attention of visitors. These communities are similar to their older neighbor in some respects, like climate, architecture, and lifestyle, yet each has its own distinctive character, attractions, and amenities. The cities closest to Palm Springs are, in order, from west to east: Cathedral City and Rancho Mirage. In

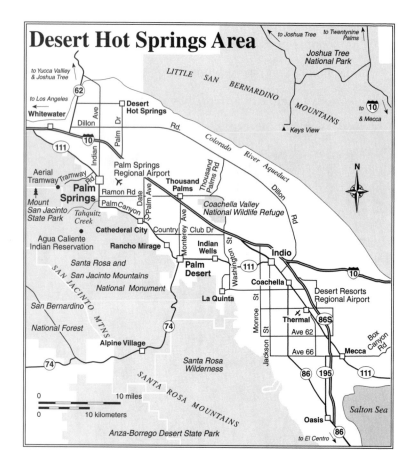

Desert Hot Springs Area

addition, a few miles north of Palm Springs, on the slope of some low, dusty hills, you'll encounter Desert Hot Springs, a once-sleepy outpost that has emerged as yet another rival for the traveler's time and attention.

Cathedral City, dubbed "Cat City" by local residents, is named after a nearby canyon whose steep, closed-in walls recall those of a grand church. This up-and-coming community immediately southeast of Palm Springs feels and looks like a place where people work and live rather than seek refuge and relax. While the actual boundary between the two cities is virtually indistinguishable, a visitor has the sense that middle-class and blue-collar wage-earners are much more at home in Cat City.

Once upon a time, before 1950, the vast desert landscape southeast of Cathedral City was dotted with horse ranches and date farms. One of the largest was named Eleven Mile Ranch, owing to its location exactly 11 miles from both Palm Springs and Indio. When developers began carving up such properties to create private estates and golf courses, they needed a name for this place. "Rancho" made

sense for obvious reasons and "Mirage" was tacked
on because of its vaguely romantic desert connota-
tions. The name stuck, and was once used by the
Ford Motor Company as the moniker for a car.

Today this exclusive haven for the walled-in rich
and retired displays so many verdant country clubs,
tall palm trees, oversized shopping centers, and
gate-locked estates as to create a kind of release
from reality. They name streets in Rancho Mirage

after such one-time residents and celebrated icons as Bob Hope, Dinah Shore, and Frank Sinatra—after a while, it seems normal.

Desert Hot Springs

About nine miles north of Palm Springs, Desert Hot Springs is a sprawling, fast-growing town perched on a hillside overlooking the west end of the Coachella Valley and the San Jacinto range. The small resorts and restaurants here are generally more moderate in prices (and amenities) than those found along the Route 111 corridor, with famous Two Bunch Palms a notable exception. Also in the mix are some retail stores, a couple of modest golf courses, and residential areas popular with retirees, families, and working singles.

The community's name derives from a large network of thermal springs that lie directly beneath it. Formed by earthquake faults, including the famous San Andreas, the water from these springs is laced with minerals and said to have great healing powers, particularly for the disabled and arthritic. Emerging from the ground at between 90 and 200 degrees Fahrenheit, most of this liquid is piped into more than three dozen small-to-medium-scale spas, many of the mom-and-pop variety. Some allow walk-in visitors to soak in their tubs and pools, others require that you be an overnight guest. As a bonus, a cool aquifer beneath the city also provides what its chamber of commerce brags is "the world's best tasting natural water."

SIGHTS

With so much going for it, the undiscovered feel of Desert Hot Springs isn't likely to last long. For tips on local happenings, contact the **Desert Hot Springs Cham-**

ber of Commerce and Visitor Information Center. ~ 11-711 West Drive; 760-329-6403; www.deserthotsprings.com, e-mail info@deserthotsprings.com

Constructed over three decades, **Cabot's Pueblo Museum** is made entirely of recycled materials, including telephone poles, railroad ties, and 135 second-hand windows. This rough-hewn palace still contains many artifacts—including a working 1882 telephone—accumulated during the life of its owner, Cabot Yerxa, who died in 1965. Also on display are ceremonial objects and other gifts given to Yerxa by friends from many Indian tribes, including those of Alaska. Overseeing the entire complex is a 43-foot-tall feathered Indian head, carved out of giant sequoia and cedar trunks by a sculptor Peter Toth. A man of many interests and talents, Yerxa was a prospector, teacher, mason, and artist who lived in Cuba and ran a cigar store in Alaska before relocating to Desert Hot Springs (20 years before it became a town) in 1913. Although he preferred a tiny, cave-like bedroom, Yerxa built the more modern upper section of the house to suit his second wife, Portia, who moved in with him in 1945. A stroll around the hillside grounds reveals whimsical signs and curiosities left by Cabot and subsequently preserved by his family and local volunteers. Now owned by

Adobe Abode

California's deserts are justifiably famous for their eccentrics. One of the oddest of the lot was homesteader Cabot Yerxa, who is credited with discovering the first of the community's hot springs while hand-digging a well here in 1914. The astonishing centerpiece of Yerxa's efforts, however, is something now called **Cabot's Pueblo Museum**, a multistoried warren of 35 asymmetrical adobe rooms built in a stacked style reminiscent of Arizona's Hopi tribe. See above for more details.

Cabot's Pueblo
Museum

the city of Desert Hot Springs, Cabot's Pueblo Museum
is closed June through September, although various special events occur here throughout the year. Open Friday
and Saturday, or Thursday by appointment. Admission.
~ 67-616 Desert View Avenue; 760-329-7610; www.
cabotsmuseum.org.

LODGING

Desert Hot Springs Spa Hotel
10-805 Palm Drive
760-329-6000, 800-808-7727
www.dhsspa.com, e-mail info@dhsspa.com
80 rooms
MODERATE TO DELUXE

Two-story guest wings enclose a courtyard with a
large swimming pool and several spring-fed hot tubs and
other soothingly warm mineral pools here. There are also
a restaurant, snack bar, bar, gift shop, and à la carte spa
on site. Rooms are basic but decent, recalling any unpretentious motel in the national chain tradition. But
you probably didn't come here to hang out in your room,

did you? Drop-in visitors can use the facilities for a fee, based on services rendered. Ask at the front desk for a list of spa and pool offerings.

Miracle Springs Resort and Spa
10625 Palm Drive
760-251-6000, 760-329-7000, 800-400-4414
www.miraclesprings.com, e-mail hotel@miraclesprings.com
50 rooms
MODERATE TO ULTRA-DELUXE

Besides the usual broad array of spa services, amenities here include six natural hot mineral pools, a big swimming pool, a "champagne bubbling" spa, saunas, and several hydrotherapy pools. One of the biggest resorts in town, though dwarfed by the mega-hotels along Route 111, the rooms are well-appointed and more lavish suites are available. There's a restaurant and lounge on site.

Two Bunch Palms Resort and Spa
67-425 Two Bunch Palms Trail
760-329-8791, 800-472-4334, fax 760-329-1317
www.twobunchpalms.com, e-mail whiteowl@twobunch
    palms.com
45 rooms
ULTRA-DELUXE

Sleep Modern

Designed by noted modernist architect John Lautner, a colleague of Frank Lloyd Wright who helped create Arizona's Taliesen West, the **Desert Hot Springs Motel** is truly unusual. The striking four-unit structure was built in 1949 and its angled concrete walls, clerestories, and glass panels are a fine example of desert modernism. Each guest room is equipped with a full kitchen, vintage furniture, replica 1940s TVs, and restored 1930s-era phones. A private patio and cactus garden extend off each room as well. Restored in 2000, the motel has no pool or spa. ~ Yerxa Road at San Antonio; 760-288-2280; www.lautnermotel.com; e-mail steve@lautnermotel.org. DELUXE.

PICTURE-PERFECT
Resort Swimming Pools

1. **Westin Mission Hills Resort,** *p. 129*
2. **Marriott's Las Palmas Resort and Spa,** *p. 129*
3. **Two Bunch Palms Resort and Spa,** *p. 110*

Two Bunch Palms is literally an oasis unto itself, a world of hot mineral baths surrounded by ancient palm trees and other native plants. This exclusive 45-acre retreat, with its guarded entrance (you must have a reservation to enter), serves as a hideaway for Hollywood celebrities and others who crave privacy. (Part of the Robert Altman movie *The Player* was filmed here.) Well-heeled folks have been visiting since the 1930s, when mobster Al Capone reputedly built the place. According to local lore, he turned this retreat into a fortress, constructing a stone house with a lookout turret and secret escape tunnel. The gangster's gambling casino has given way to a health-oriented gourmet restaurant and his ultra-secure hideout has become a laid-back resort. Guests soak in the hot mineral pools, utilize a sophisticated spa facility with saunas and massage therapists, and wander an estate that includes lawns, tennis courts, swimming pool, nude sunbathing areas, and koi ponds. Choose from luxurious guest rooms, casitas, and villas, or the exclusive "House on the Hill." Some connoisseurs insist that this is the most romantic and exclusive of all area resorts. Closed the last week of August. Adults only.

DINING

Restaurants at several Desert Hot Springs resorts, including Miracle Springs Resort and Desert Hot Springs Spa Hotel, are open to the public. Inquire about daily specials and Sunday brunch. For the most part, restaurants in Desert Hot Springs are unexceptional and you are better off driving to Palm Springs if you want a special dining experience.

Kam Lum
66610 8th Street
760-251-1244
closed Monday
BUDGET TO MODERATE

This modest Chinese eatery, set in a mini-mall, serves standard Cantonese dishes such as orange beef and shrimp with lobster sauce, as well as a dozen specialty dishes. The food is good, the portions generous, and the service just fine, even if the decor is less than inspiring.

La Palapa
11-349 Palm Drive
760-288-3315
MODERATE

This is a good Mexican restaurant, with 11-piece mariachi bands livening up the place on weekend nights. Particularly recommended are the generous combination plates (i.e. enchiladas and tacos), washed down with delicious margaritas. The palm-shaded patio is a pleasant place for outdoor dining.

SHOPPING

There's not much to shop for here beyond the standard stuff and a few worthy second-hand stores. The latter include **Revivals** (12975 Palm Drive; 760-329-0845), offering quality antiques, consignments, and furnishings with sales supporting local AIDS-related services, and **A Dollar or Less** (14180 Palm Drive; 760-251-7759), where there are some real finds for under a buck. The larger hotels and resorts have well-stocked gift shops where you can pick up desert-oriented clothing and accessories.

During mid-October, the citywide **Festival of the Waters** brings arts and crafts to the streets along with music, food, dance, and entertainment. On Friday and Saturday, from October to June, you can shop at the art gallery, trading post, and gem shop situated at **Cabot's**

Pueblo Museum. ~ 67-616 Desert View Avenue; 760-329-7610.

NIGHTLIFE

Your best bets are found in hotel-based restaurants and a scattering of local restaurants or lounges. Try **Chuck-walla's** at Miracle Springs. ~ 10625 Palm Drive; 760-251-6000. Or stop by **Sunshine Sports Bar** at Desert Hot Springs Spa Hotel ~ Yerxa Road at San Antonio; 760-288-2280.

There's live music by local musicians on weekends at **Tommy's Nightclub.** ~ 12-520 Palm Drive; 760-251-1045. **La Palapa** features authentic Mexican mariachi music on the weekends as well. ~ 11-349 Palm Drive; 760-288-3315.

Cathedral City If Palm Springs is where the

wealthy let their hair down, Cathedral City is where those who serve them roll their shirtsleeves up. According to its Chamber of Commerce, the population of this on-the-go community is 49 percent Hispanic and about 30 percent gay or lesbian, with one in five businesses owned and operated by women. Here you'll see glass-and-steel office parks, tract-style subdivisions, family-oriented shopping centers, and boxy warehouses. However, you will also find some worthy diversions, including fine restaurants, unique stores, attractive golf courses, and praiseworthy lodging. A colorful, pedestrian-friendly town square anchors a civic center, with an enormous, whimsically sculpted fountain as a centerpiece, where community celebrations are held throughout the year.

SIGHTS

There are some gems amid the dross of Cathedral City's business parks, industrial strips, and cookie-cutter housing developments. You'll have to look carefully, but they are worth the search. For assistance, contact the **Cathedral City Chamber of Commerce.** ~ 760-328-7333, 760-328-1213; www.cathedralcitycc.com.

The Cat City movie and restaurant complex called he **Mary Pickford Theater & Salon** is aptly named, for it houses a small museum honoring the life of the celebrated 1920s-era actress, one of the first Hollywood stars to have (with her actor husband, Douglas Fairbanks) a winter home in the Palm Springs area. On display are personal items donated by Pickford's family, including the actress's 1976 lifetime achievement Oscar and a gorgeous gown she wore in the 1927 film, "Dorothy Vernon of Haddon Hall." Two informative biographical videos are shown, including one produced by Pickford. ~ 36-850 Pickfair Street; 760-328-7100.

Cathedral City is also the final resting place for some very well-known personalities. At **Desert Memorial Park** you can visit the grave of singer Frank Sinatra, flanked by his parents beneath a headstone that reads "The Best Is Yet To Come." Nearby lies singer-songwriter (and former Palms Springs mayor and congressman) Sonny Bono, who fatally collided with a tree while skiing in 1998. Leading man William Powell, star of *The Thin Man* and many other films, is here, along with the shy Gabor sister Magda and over-the-top 1930s director Busby Berkeley. Two beloved songwriters are buried in this cemetery: Frederick Loewe and James Van Heusen. Surprisingly, Desert Memorial Park is also the site of the **Gay Veterans Memorial**, this country's only public monument exclusively honoring gay, lesbian, bisexual, and transgender veterans who gave their lives during U.S. military service. ~ 31705 DeVall Drive at Ramon Drive; 760-328-3316.

Watching an IMAX film is a thrill like nothing else. Shot on unusually wide film stock these specialty films are projected with impeccable visual detail and pristine

Mary Pickford Theater & Salon

sound quality on a screen six-stories high. Sitting in stadium-style seats and surrounded by high-fidelity speakers, you feel totally immersed in the experience. Check it out at the **Desert IMAX Theatre**, a family-friendly venue showing such G-rated fare as *The Lion King, Fighter Pilot, Ocean Oasis,* and *Nascar 3D*. Admission. ⌐ 68510 East Palm Canyon Drive; 760-324-7333; www. desertimax.com.

Fun for kids of all ages awaits at **Camelot Park Family Entertainment Center**, an indoor/outdoor complex featuring a wide variety of video games, arcade competitions, bumper boats, batting cages, go-carts, laser tag, and miniature golf (get 'em started while they're young!).

Desert Memorial Park   There's a separate fee for each activity. ~ 67-700 East Palm Canyon Drive; 760-770-7532.

LODGING

Accommodations in Cathedral City are more limited than in neighboring Palm Springs, but there are plenty of national chains represented (not detailed here) as well as a nice spectrum of small-to-large independent hotels. Cat City has the advantage of being near Palm Springs International Airport and a bit closer to the Down Valley shopping and golf attractions. As in Palm Springs, there are a number of gay-friendly hostelries here.

Ambiente Inn
37112 Palo Verde
760-770-1697, fax 760-770-8756
www.ambienteinn.com, e-mail mail@ambienteinn.com
13 rooms
MODERATE TO DELUXE

The spacious rooms of this renovated, stylish Fifties-era motel include full kitchens, private patios, Internet access, and DVD players. Each room has a theme corresponding to one of the seven continents, including Antarctica. There are two pools, a 10-person spa, and the grounds are clothing optional. An expanded continental breakfast is complimentary, along with a Saturday evening barbecue. Gay-male exclusively. Adjacent is an all-gay, 6-room "fetish and fantasy" annex called The Black Palm.

If You Build It . . .

Cat City has turned Field of Dreams into a reality. The fictional Hollywood movie was based on the improbable belief of one determined man, played by Kevin Costner, that if he built an old-fashioned major league baseball field at his Iowa farm, the sport's greatest athletes would come there to play. At **Big League Dreams Sports Park** (one of several in California) you can attend a softball game or use a batting cage at downsized replicas of New York's Yankee Stadium, Boston's Fenway Park, and Chicago's Wrigley Field. Most usage comes from local amateur leagues, but sometimes everyday fans really do get to play here with their life-long heroes. Yes, if someone builds it, they will

come. Sports other than baseball are played here, too, including in-line hockey, basketball, flag football, sand volleyball, and soccer. Admission to some events and attractions. ~ 33-700 Date Palm Drive; 760-324-5600, 888-390-7275; www.bigleaguedreams.com.

Doral Palm Springs Resort
67-967 Vista Chino
760-322-7000, fax 760-322-6853
www.doralpalmsprings.com
285 rooms
DELUXE

Golfers and other outdoor enthusiasts are especially catered to at this luxurious, four-story resort. Here, you have immediate access to 27 PGA Championship holes plus entrance to the 36-hole, links-style Cimarron Country Club next door. There are also tennis courts and spa facilities on site, along with a 5000-square-foot pool, snack bar, and lounge. Rooms are spacious and the suites include living rooms; all have high-speed Internet access.

Desert Princess Country Club Hotel
28822 Desert Princess Drive
760-322-3378, fax 760-327-9699
www.desertprincesscc.com
100 rooms
DELUXE

For those who plan to stay awhile, one- to three-bedroom condos with full kitchens, private patios, and living rooms are available at this country club locale, which features easy access to two golf courses, two putting greens

Just Like Mom Used to Make (Well, Almost)

Portions are huge, the comfort food delicious, the coffee endless, and breakfast available from 6 a.m. until 2 p.m. at **Don & Sweet Sue's Café**, an eclectic, warmhearted diner. They serve lunch and dinner, too, with an eye toward recipes your mom might have used, with some 21st-century flourishes added. Try the buttermilk pancakes at breakfast and the cheeseburgers at lunch. The down-home meat loaf might even be better than mom's. ~ 68-955 Ramon Road; 760-770-2760. BUDGET TO MODERATE.

(one over 10,000-square-feet in size), several tennis courts, pools, fitness center, driving range, and spa. The grounds sprawl over 250 well-manicured acres. The condos are privately owned and nicely furnished—but you came here to play golf, right?

DINING

El Gallito
68-820 Grove Street
760-328-7794
closed Monday
BUDGET TO MODERATE

This cheap, funky, fun, bare-bones café offers great south-of-the-border food at even better prices. There are piñatas and hokey velvet paintings on the walls, and

some talented people back in the kitchen. The crowd is local, ingredients are fresh, and the menu is solid if not predictable.

Oceans Oyster Bar and Grill
67555 East Palm Canyon Drive
760-324-1554
MODERATE TO DELUXE

It's a long way to the coast, but the air-shipped seafood is fresh and special at this friendly and inviting place, tucked into an ordinary-looking shopping mall. From the lobster ravioli to the calamari arrabiata, every dish here pleases the palate. And, yes, there are oysters.

 SHOPPING

Major shopping centers are in the planning stages, but as this book went to press this remained a community whose residents drove elsewhere for their major shopping. That said, Cathedral City does have several specialty stores sure to delight the budget-minded. At **Little**

Baja you will find Mexican pottery, wall masks, statuary, and pottery reproductions of pre-Columbian idols. ~ 34-750 Date Palm Drive; 760-328-3708.

A hidden treasure, the **Palm Springs Candy Company** makes candy completely by hand, using time-tested recipes dating back to 1942. From chocolate-dipped Medjool dates to honey-macadamia-nut corn, you'll be sure to find a sweet you can't wait to eat. ~ 68-845 Perez Road, Suite H-11; 760-321-1231; www.palmsprings candy.com.

Perez Plaza, is home to several budget-priced specialty shops of interest to the discriminating shopper. **Imposter Purses Etc.** (760-202-1866) sells designer look-alike purses and jewelry (inspired by Gucci, Louis Vuitton, Hermes, and others); **I.V. Etc.** (760-321-8429) is a purveyor of fine pima cotton robes, sleepwear, and casual clothes; and **Designer Shoes & Clothing** (760-324-4477) focuses on fashionable women's shoes, apparel, and accessories. ~ 67-895 Perez Road.

Upscale Resale

On what is informally referred to as Resale Row, a string of shops tucked into an unremarkable industrial park house some incredible antiques, vintage furniture, new housewares, and second-hand goods, including clothing and jewelry. The cream of the crop may be **Dromos: The Road to Design** (760-328-8228), which specializes in exquisite new lighting, furniture, art objects, and Asian religious statuary. Also worth a close look are the adjacent **Furniture Recycling**, with new, used, vintage, and one-of-a-kind furniture, art, accessories, and tchotkes (760-324-6546); **Revivals**, widely considered the highest-quality used-clothing and collectibles store in the area, where all sales benefit AIDS programs (760-328-1330); and **The Litter Box** (760-321-8205), where profits from upscale resale furnishings and other items support a local SPCA chapter. ~ 68-929 Perez Road.

NIGHTLIFE

A spirited bar and dinner theater, **Wilde Goose Cabaret** offers an unusual assortment of nightly entertainment that includes comedy, harp music, jazz, Broadway hits, and drag shows (though not all at the same time). They serve equally diverse, deluxe-priced cuisine and Sunday brunch. Occasional cover charge. ~ 67-938 East Palm Canyon Drive; 760-328-5775.

The gay-friendly **Poolside Bar** in the Desert Palms Inn features nightly entertainment ranging from cabaret-style productions to local music acts. Occasional cover. ~ 67-580 East Palm Canyon Drive; 760-324-3000; www.desertpalmsinn.com.

Ground Zero is a lively bar and nightclub for gay men offering karaoke, dancing, drag shows, and pool tournaments. There are occasional live bands as well as deejays. Occasional cover. ~ 36737 Cathedral Canyon Drive; 760-321-0031.

Rancho Mirage
Sometimes called "the playground of the presidents," Rancho Mirage has played host to nearly every U.S. commander in chief since Eisenhower, and Gerald Ford has a busy boulevard named after him. Such power brokers were often hosted by the late philanthropist, business tycoon, and onetime ambassador Walter Annenberg, who entertained many heads of state here and once offered asylum to the deposed Shah of Iran's mother and sister. This is where Ronald and Nancy Reagan spent every New Year's Eve during the Reagan Administration. And why not? Annenberg's 205-estate, Sunnylands, boasted a huge mansion, a nine-hole golf course, and 12 artificial ponds.

Despite the natural heat and aridity, water is used here everywhere—for fountains, cascades, fairways—in a splendid display of carefree excess. You often can see some of this greenery on national television, since many top golf tournaments are broadcast from local courses. (The electric golf cart was developed at Rancho Mirage's Thunderbird Country Club, the area's first golf course, built in the 1940s.) Sometimes peninsular desert bighorn sheep, an endangered species, are lured down from the hills to munch on all this foliage, which explains the Bighorn Sheep Crossing signs you may notice along Route 111. The bighorn has also been adopted as the community's official symbol.

Lest you think Rancho Mirage is all about money, its city government has spent funds on affordable housing, a large library, and a peaceful patch of greenery called

Betty Ford Center

A haven for those seeking discreet and effective treatment for drug and alcohol addictions, this facility is not open to the public. My friend, Laurie, refers to this unquestioned practice as "the hush-hush on the who's who." Although popular with the wealthy, celebrated, and powerful, the center keeps a low profile. It derives its name from the former First Lady and Rancho Mirage resident, who had her own alcohol addiction treated at the Long Beach Naval Hospital in Long Beach before co-founding this rehab unit in 1982. Committed to Betty Ford's vision of a facility attuned to women's needs, the center makes sure that half its clients are female and that its treatment is family-oriented. You may find something ironic about a place where a former occupant of the White House and self-described recovering alcoholic lends her name to promote an exclusive rehab center for society's upper-crust, but that's part of Rancho Mirage's unique charm. ~ 39-000 Bob Hope Drive; 760-773-4100; www.bettyfordcenter.org.

Cancer Survivor Park. There's also a highly regarded medical center named after, you guessed it, Dwight Eisenhower.

SIGHTS

Rancho Mirage will not likely be accused of being the most family-friendly city in the world—one suspects that the children of many residents are at least middle-aged—but if the grandkids visit there's more for them to do than watch video games or practice their golf swings. For local information contact the **Rancho Mirage Chamber of Commerce.** ~ 42-464 Rancho Mirage Lane; 760-568-9351; www.ranchomirage.org. The **Palm Springs Desert**

Resorts Convention and Visitors Authority also has an outpost here, providing extensive information on attractions and services in the surrounding communities. Closed weekends. ~ 70-100 Route 111, Rancho Mirage; 760-770-9000, 800-967-3767; www.palmspringsusa.com.

More than 50 hands-on exhibits for inquisitive young people are available at the refreshingly creative **Children's Discovery Museum of the Desert**. Eschewing the "don't touch" dictum of most museums, this place invites its visitors to climb a big rock, sort out the bones of a skeleton, work with hand tools, dress up in an attic, splash paint on a VW bug, shop at a grocery, or make a sculp-

Children's Discovery Museum of the Desert

ture on a magnetic wall. Other hands-on options include Dig It, an honest-to-goodness archaeological site where kids can unearth actual Cahuilla Indian artifacts, with an informed docent to supervise. There's also an outdoor amphitheater, gift shop, covered picnic area, and performing arts center that offers early childhood education programs. It's an unforgettable adventure that most area visitors never seem to learn about. Closed Monday from May through December. Admission. ~ 71-701 Gerald Ford Drive; 760-321-0602; www.cdmod.org.

LODGING

The Lodge at Rancho Mirage
68-900 Frank Sinatra Drive
760-321-8282, 800-241-3333, fax 760-321-8997
www.rockresorts.com
300 rooms
DELUXE TO ULTRA-DELUXE

Guests staying in any of the accommodations here (formerly the Ritz-Carlton Rancho Mirage) have only to open the French doors to their patio or balcony to enjoy a commanding view of the entire Coachella Valley. Perched on a 650-foot-high plateau in the Santa Rosa Mountain foothills, this is an *über*-lavish 24-acre hotel and tennis resort. Fine original art, custom fabrics, antiques, crown moldings, and other luxury-level amenities are standard in each room and the spacious suites are truly elegant. There are three excellent restaurants, 10 tennis courts, boutiques, and a spa, along with many other upscale features including a swimming pool and sun deck surrounded by tall palm trees. As you'd expect, service is first-rate.

PICTURE-PERFECT
Places to Cool Off

1. **Desert Hot Springs Spa Hotel, Desert Hot Springs, *p. 109***
2. **Desert IMAX Theatre, Cathedral City, *p. 117***
3. **River at Rancho Mirage, *p. 131***

Marriott's Las Palmas Resort and Spa

41-000 Bob Hope Drive
760-568-2727, 800-458-8786, fax 760-862-4565
www.rancholaspalmas.com
472 rooms
DELUXE TO ULTRA-DELUXE

More family-oriented than many of the area's other luxury destination-style resorts, a Spanish Colonial theme prevails throughout this 240-acre facility. Guests have access to a 27-hole golf course, 25 tennis courts, four restaurants, a convention center, spa, health club, beauty salon, children's programs, and many other perks. The resort is admired for its three large swimming pools, the biggest with a 100-foot waterslide. All of the Mission-style rooms are unusually spacious and have sitting areas, private patios or balconies, along with motif-appropriate furnishings and stunning views.

Westin Mission Hills Resort

71-333 Dinah Shore Drive
760-328-5955, 800-228-3000, fax 760-321-2607
www.westin.com, e-mail ranch@westin.com
512 rooms
DELUXE TO ULTRA-DELUXE

A true haven for the golf and tennis crowd, this Moroccan-style resort sits on 360 acres, surrounded by fairways (designed by Pete Dye and Gary Player), putting greens, and your choice of clay or grass courts. Families are welcome; there are professional babysitters as well as special programs for guests aged four through twelve. Besides the meandering artificial streams, there are three swimming pools—one of them a virtual lagoon with a water slide 60 feet high. Guest rooms are large and meticulously appointed in a subdued, artfully elegant manner. On the grounds or adjacent are several restaurants, two 18-hole golf courses, seven tennis courts, a spa, salon, convention center, and volleyball court, among other goodies.

Restaurant Row

A short stretch of Route 111 (also known as East Palm Canyon Drive) through Rancho Mirage has earned the moniker Restaurant Row. There are more than 30 dining establishments between Frank Sinatra Drive and Bob Hope Drive serving everything from gourmet hot dogs to sumptuous haute cuisine. Included in the mouth-watering melange are specialists in Hawaiian fusion, French, Pacific Rim, Continental, Greek, Italian, Thai, and California cuisine.

The most choices along Rancho Mirage's Restaurant Row are found at The River at Rancho Mirage, a 30-acre shopping center with a faux river and waterfront (of course). Here you can park your car, take a short walk, and choose from among a number of popular eating establishments, including P.F. Chang's China Bistro, Fleming's Prime Steakhouse, Babe's Bar-B-Que & Brewery, Maki Maki Sushi Bar, and Il Tango. ~ 71-800 Route 111; 760-341-2711; www.theriveratranchomirage.com.

DINING

Las Casuelas Nuevas
70050 Route 111
760-328-8844
Sunday brunch
MODERATE TO ULTRA-DELUXE

A spectacular Mexican restaurant disguised as a Spanish Colonial hacienda, this is part of a small local chain that has been drawing rave reviews (and loyal customers) for more than 40 years. Strolling mariachis and flamenco guitarists complement the delicious rendering of Mexico's classic cuisine. Specialties include *pollo en mole*, crab enchiladas, and spicy port fajitas. The Sunday champagne brunch is particularly memorable. Sit on the garden patio or in the *mas elegante* dining room.

SHOPPING

The River at Rancho Mirage is a classy local shopping landmark providing food, movies, live entertainment, wine tastings, and other special events as well as featuring retailers selling everything from handmade chocolate truffles to trend-setting designer eyewear. And, yes, at the heart of it all there is a (human-made) river, complete with colonnade-shaded waterfront restaurants and pleasing music occasionally wafting from an adjacent amphitheater. The park-like setting is enhanced by cascading waterfalls and dancing fountains. ~ Between Bob Hope Drive and Rancho Las Palmas at 71-800 Route 111; 760-341-2711; www.theriveratranchomirage.com.

One of the lesser-known jewels of The River shopping complex is **Water's Edge Gallery**, a fitting showcase for some of the most acclaimed West Coast contemporary fine art painters. Such artists as Sally Rosenbaum, Dan Fogel, Mikki Senkarik, and Michael Godard have exhibited here; their work ranges from abstract to representational, landscapes to human figures. ~ 71800 Route 111, Suite A-140; 760-836-0922.

The popular **Lady Golf & Resort Apparel** chain is based in Rancho Mirage and shoppers at its flagship store will find a premier selection of stylish women's shoes, sportswear, and accessories, all offered at good prices. ~ 42412 Bob Hope Drive; 760-773-4949.

Another women's apparel store that merits attention is **7th Avenue West**, selling prestigious designer clothing at discounted prices, with new merchandise arriving daily. Check out the top-label pants and dyed-to-match blouses and sweaters. ~ 72-060 Route 111; 760-340-6555.

Blame It On Midnight

With mauve brocade booths, a misted terrace, and a giant granite slab for a bar, **Shame on the Moon** is both elegant and modern, with an old-fashioned ambience and exemplary service. This visually stunning dining room maintains debonair standards and you'll want to dress up a bit. The menu is eclectic and portions are large. Diners may feast on the special entrées whipped up each evening, based on a menu that changes seasonally to take advantage of fresh fruit and vegetables. Continental dishes range from baked filet of salmon with a fresh horseradish crust to orange-glazed duck. Desserts, like everything else here, are prepared with utmost care, made from scratch on the premises. An intense three-layer chocolate cake is a permanent fixture on the menu. Dinner only. Closed mid-July to mid-August. ~ 69-950 Frank Sinatra Drive; 760-324-5515, fax 760-770-4654. MODERATE TO ULTRA-DELUXE.

The Luxury Resort Tradition

Even if you're staying in smaller or more modest digs, you owe it to yourself to at least take a look at the scale of luxury that exists at the larger resorts in the Rancho Mirage area. Although most of the amenities are not available to non-paying guests, you are usually welcome to stop for a drink, a meal, or a stroll around the grounds. Some resorts make golf, tennis, swimming, fitness equipment, and spa facilities available to outsiders on a pay-for-use basis. Call ahead and ask the concierge for details. The inclusive nature of these cushy destinations reflect a trend in the Coachella Valley—and the travel industry in general—toward offering a place where you can be pampered to your heart's content without leaving the compound. In this self-contained world, you can forget about what lies beyond the resort's boundaries. Thus, what began here as a tradition of offering luxury exclusively to the rich and famous has been democratized, with anyone with the financial means able to enjoy delights previously reserved for potentates, moguls, and movie stars. Of course, if all you do is want to lounge by the pool and read a book, they'll let you do that, too.

Mixed in with the automobile dealers and restaurants along Route 111, Rancho Mirage's main drag, you'll find a broad assortment of specialty retailers offering high-quality home furnishings and accessories. Slow down and take a look.

NIGHTLIFE

The **Agua Caliente Casino**, the newer of two gaming ventures operated by the local Agua Caliente tribe, presents a wide array of Las Vegas–style gaming: slots, video poker, bingo, blackjack, stud, mini-baccarat, and more. The brightly lit complex includes a 1000-seat showroom and a smaller performance space, along with several bars and six restaurants featuring everything from pizza slices to prime rib. The casino's **Canyons Lounge** has free live entertainment, running the gamut from two-step to salsa, rock to swing. Some nights include complimentary dance lessons. ~ 32-250 Bob Hope Drive; 760-321-2000; www.hotwatercasino.com.

If piano music is your thing, high thee to **Wally's Desert Turtle** (71-775 Route 111; 760-568-9321), a

Hot, Hot, Hot

For fans of salsa, cumbia, merengue, cha cha, and other kinds of Latin dancing, **Caramba's Musicantina** comes to life with a picante and infectious
beat every night at 10 p.m. There's a full bar, two dance floors, and (in a
separate part of the building) a terrific Mexican restaurant. Cover. ~ 70050
Route 111; 760-328-8844.

continental restaurant that also features fashion show
luncheons on Friday, November through May. Other
Rancho Mirage restaurants with live entertainment one
or more nights a week include **Haleiwa Joe's Seafood
Grill** (69-934 Route 111; 760-324-5613) and **Kobe Japanese Steakhouse** (69-838 Route 111; 760-324-1717),
along with the lounges at Westin Mission Hills Resort
and The Lodge at Rancho Mirage. Covers vary.

At **The River at Rancho Mirage**, the city's mammoth
shopping center, you'll find a 12-screen movie complex
and an outdoor amphitheater that has occasional live entertainment, mainly during cooler months. ~ 71800 Route
111; 760-341-2711; www.theriveratranchomirage.com.

PARKS

As the Coachella Valley rapidly filled with people, roads,
and buildings during the 1980s, it became clear to scientists, nature lovers, and other concerned individuals
that decisive action had to be taken if any of the basin's
most fragile and unusual desert habitat was to be saved.
In 1986, about 21,000 acres in the Indio Hills, on the
northern edge of the valley, were legally protected
through formation of the **Coachella Valley Preserve**. The

greatest treasure encompassed in this rolling parkland is cool, green Thousand Palms Oasis, a singular ecosystem that features not only hundreds of palm trees, but springs, ponds, and waterways that are home to rare pupfish, holdovers from Ancient Lake Cahuilla found in only

a few other locations. The preserve also protects a fragment of the wind-blown sand dunes that once covered 100 square miles of the valley, now reduced to less than five percent of that amount. These dunes are the only place on Earth where the extremely endangered Coachella Valley fringe-toed lizard is found. Amazingly well adapted to this environment, this species has evolved to "swim" through the sand on toes that provide quick getaways from excessive heat as well as predators. The largest of three separate units (the other two are north of Palm Springs), the approximately 17,000 acres surrounding Thousand Palms Oasis and nearby Mc-Callum Grove (along with 11 smaller oases) is the site of a rustic visitors center and picnic area, as well as a well-maintained network of hiking and riding trails. All sorts of birds, lizards, snakes, rodents, spiders, bats, and small mammals may be observed here. Guided tours by volunteer docents can be arranged by calling ahead. Oversight of the reserve is by the nonprofit Center for Natural Lands Management in cooperation with various government agencies. Open daily sunrise to sunset, except in August. The visitors center operates from 8 a.m. to noon. ~ about 15 miles east of Palm Springs via Ramon and Thousand Palms Canyon Roads; 760-343-2733, 760-343-1234.

4.

Palm Desert
Area

A dozen miles east of Palm Springs on Route 111, prosperous Palm Desert emerged during the 1990s as the unchallenged "in" destination for Coachella Valley visitors. This sleek upstart has displaced its more staid rivals in the eyes of many travelers as the place they most want to shop, dine, play, and relax. Palm Desert is much more than a fashionable address, however, as evidenced by its impressive commitment to the arts and support of a fine outdoor nature museum. Although many of its amenities carry an eye-popping price tag, there's still something here for everyone.

Even more upper-crust is Palm Desert's "Down Valley" neighbor, Indian Wells. This low-profile town long has boasted a median household income well into six figures, a median age near 60, and an estimated three-fourths of all residents living behind locked gates. Since its incorporation in 1967, Indian Wells has dominated the Top Ten List of per-capita income for California communities. Microsoft founder Bill Gates is one of several billionaires maintaining a home here.

Just south of Indian Wells and tucked into a cove-like pocket that's almost completely surrounded by barren mountains, La Quinta has grown from a tiny, sleepy village to a sprawling residential area dominated by championship golf courses and one of the area's largest leisure complexes. La Quinta Resort & Club opened in 1927 as a quiet getaway destination for big names in Hollywood and business. Famed movie director Frank Capra, for in-

stance, wrote his screenplay for *It Happened One Night* and other classics while staying here.

The easternmost city in the urban chain that extends east from Palm Springs is humble Indio, a low-to-middle-income residential zone established to serve an important rail hub and agricultural interests that include numerous date farms. Its attractions include casinos, nationally known polo facilities, and several quirky winter festivals.

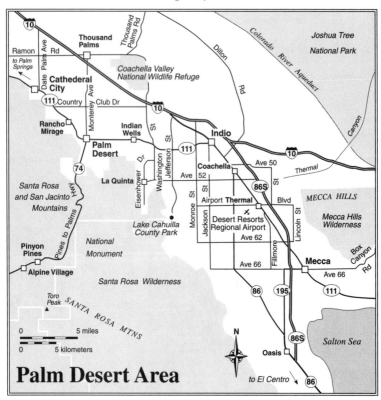

Palm Desert Area

Palm Desert

The thriving business, shopping, and residential community of Palm Desert, just beyond Rancho Mirage, has much to offer the affluent retail-minded traveler. The city's upscale El Paseo district, for example, is now world-famous as the mecca for discriminating, well-heeled shoppers. Nearby, Westfield Shoppingtown is a magnet for commerce that attracts patrons from near and far. These two areas kick-started development here in the 1960s and again in the 1980s.

Besides boutiques and country clubs, Palm Desert visitors can take in a superb zoo and one of the area's quirkiest annual events, November's fun-loving Golf Cart Parade. Indeed, golf carts are so well-loved here that a city ordinance makes them "street legal" as an incentive for resident convenience and energy conservation. In the same spirit, the city-owned Desert Willow Golf Course is a pioneer in the use of water-thrifty, drought-tolerant landscaping.

As in other desert communities, most land in Palm Desert is devoted to low-slung private homes and commercial development. As you drive through the city, you may wonder where people congregate, outside of churches and shopping districts. Look closely, and you'll find some exceptions.

SIGHTS

Palm Desert is an important education and arts center for the Coachella Valley. It is home to the College of the Desert, a public community college, and McCallum Theater for the Performing Arts, the largest and most sophisticated facility of its kind hereabouts. As part of an ongoing effort to actively support the arts, a city-spon-

Desert Holocaust Memorial

sored public art initiative has placed more than 100 pieces of sculpture in highly visible locations along El Paseo and in **Civic Center Park**. The park is a 72-acre property dotted with 23 artworks set among rose gardens, municipal buildings, a lake, a jogging path, and tennis and basketball courts. Be sure to check out Ben Watling's playful *Coyote Benches* and S. Seward Johnson Jr.'s hyper-realistic *Midstream*. ~ Fred Waring Drive and San Pablo Avenue; 760-568-9697.

Learn more or get art tour maps by contacting or stopping by the **Palm Desert Visitor Information Center.** ~ 72-990 Route 111, between Fred Waring Drive and Magnesia Falls Drive; 760-568-1441, 800-873-2428; www.palm-desert.org.

Straddling the border between Palm Desert and Indian Wells, the appropriately named **Living Desert** is a 1200-acre zoo and botanical garden that presents a raw

and realistic picture of life in an arid environment. Th
beautifully designed, animal-friendly facility contains
raffes, gazelles, warthogs, oryx, and many other animals
native to African deserts. There are special displays housing non-releasable predatory birds, tortoises, and geckos,
and walk-through aviaries that are home to finches, green
herons, hermit thrushes, and hummingbirds. The Eagle
Canyon section, a wildlife exhibit and endangered
species breeding center, is home to mountain lions, bobcats, coyotes, wolves, and golden eagles, among other animals. Village WaTuTu features leopards, camels, hyenas,
and a "petting Kraal." There are also botanical gardens
with vegetation from eight of the world's deserts, and
hiking trails that wind for more than six miles into
nearby foothills. Ponds re-create life at an oasis, and a
wildlife hospital provides a close-up look at animals re-
ceiving medical care. This exceptional park delivers a
strong conservation message while also providing such
amenities as restaurants, an artist in residence, a gift

In Tribute

The Palm Desert Civic Center Park is home to the **Desert Holocaust Memorial**, created through the efforts of the local Desert Holocaust Committee, whose members include individuals who were targets of the Nazi extermination campaigns of World War II. Erected as a reminder of those horrific events and a tribute to both its victims and survivors, the monument is dominated by seven oversized bronze figures, whose faces are modeled after some of those captured news photographs. The figures are mounted on a double-tiered Star of David and surrounded by cobblestones and lighting that recall the Auschwitz concentration camp. A circle of trees around the perimeter represents life beyond imprison-ment. ~ Fred Waring Drive at San Pablo Avenue; 760-325-7281; www.palm-desert.org/holocaust.

shop, shuttle service, and fun holiday events for kids. Reduced hours mid-June through August. Admission. ~ 47-900 Portola Avenue; 760 346-5694, fax 760-568-9685; www.livingdesert.org.

LODGING

Marriott's Desert Springs Resort and Spa
74-855 Country Club Drive
760-341-2211, 800-228-9290, fax 760-341-1872
www.desertspringsresort.com
900 rooms
ULTRA-DELUXE

Marriott's Desert Springs Resort and Spa

The ultimate expression of the area's water profligacy is found at Marriott's Desert Springs Resort and Spa, an opulent 450-acre resort featuring hanging gardens, five-tiered waterfalls, an eight-story atrium, 21 tennis courts, two golf courses, a shopping arcade, a beauty salon, and

Southwestern Comfort

A block away from El Paseo on a quiet residential street, the comfortable, low-key **Tres Palmas Bed & Breakfast** is nicely accented with Navajo rugs, tile floors, an open-beam ceiling, and other Southwestern elements. The four guest rooms are large and furnished in a style that recalls Santa Fe or Sedona. A homemade continental breakfast is complimentary, as are afternoon drinks and snacks. There's a pool and hot tub, too. ~ 73-135 Tumbleweed Lane; 760-773-9858, 800-770-9858, fax 760-776-9159. DELUXE.

---

a palm-fringed lagoon with gondolas and other water-craft. There are lovely crystalline lakes—all artificial—and one of the five swimming pools is a 12,000-square-foot extravaganza that is both indoor and outdoor. Think Versailles—or Venice—in the desert. It comes as no surprise that the deluxe spa alone takes up 30,000 square feet. Rooms, each with a private patio or balcony, are well furnished and commodious.

Hotel Mojave
73721 Shadow Mountain Drive
760-346-6121, 800-391-1104, fax 760-674-9072
www.hotelmojave.com, e-mail jr@broughtonhospitality.com
24 rooms
DELUXE TO ULTRA-DELUXE

Mere steps away from the chic shops, beauty salons, and fine restaurants on El Paseo, this boutique hotel seeks to re-create the glamour, romance, and sophistication of the 1940s with vintage furnishings and other special touches consistent with its flash-from-the-past theme. A deluxe continental breakfast is complimentary and each room has a minibar, retro video library, and private patio. Some Mojave accommodations have kitchenettes and fireplaces. There's also an on-location spa as well as a pool and tranquil courtyard, while an off-site health club is available to all guests.

DINING

Palm Desert has no Restaurant Row in the Rancho Mirage tradition, but it is a wonderful city in which to dine. There's no shortage of fine restaurants in seemingly endless variety, with the emphasis on Continental, French, and steakhouse cuisines. Most eateries are clustered along Route 111 and in the streets immediately parallel in either direction, Fred Waring Drive and El Paseo. In a community where shopping has been elevated to an art form, malls like Westfield (located at Monterey Drive and Route 111) harbor some excellent dining spots as well.

Louise's Pantry
4491 Town Center Way
760 346-9320
breakfast and lunch only
BUDGET TO MODERATE

Everybody's favorite lunch counter is found at Louise's Pantry, a landmark café so popular with the locals that they often line up outside the door. This is a plastic-and-formica eatery where the matronly waitresses are the real thing—and always call you "hon." They seem genuinely pleased to deliver hot coffee and standard but high-quality American diner fare. Settle into a booth, pull up a counter stool, or relax on patio and sample meat loaf, pork chops, or filet of sole. The fresh, homemade soup is recommended as are the daily entrée specials. Save room for the made-from-scratch pie.

Marriott Boat Tours

The Venetian gondolas at Marriott's Desert Springs Resort and Spa have more than a decorative purpose. After you check in, one will transport you in style from the glass-walled lobby to your

room. In the evening, a gondolier will pole you to whichever on-site restaurant you've chosen. During the morning, you can float to any of more than a dozen boutiques. And if you'd like simply to show up and take a sightseeing tour, well, that can be arranged—or you can join one of the guided excursions that's scheduled every afternoon. These are open to outside visitors as well as hotel guests. As you glide along the glittering waterways, you may hear the tropical calypso music of a steel drum band or delight in watching the exotic parrots, macaws, and cockatoos that share the lobby atrium with visitors. Outside, there are pink flamingos and regal swans strutting their stuff. It's all a bit unreal, but that's the point here, isn't it?

The Inn on El Paseo
73-445 El Paseo
760-340-1236, fax 760-340-2624
weekend brunch
MODERATE TO DELUXE

The Inn on El Paseo is a little old-fashioned, in a cozy and soothing way, which might be the reason it has such a loyal following among local residents. White walls, flowery curtains, and oak booths are a trademark here, along with gracious service. The cuisine, as you might expect, is generous and straight-arrow American, with such dependable entrées as fresh salmon, beef medallions, Cobb salad, and rack of lamb. The desserts are homemade and there's a full bar. Dine inside or take advantage

Vegetarian Delight

If you think you know (or want to know) about scrumptious vegetarian cooking, you need to experience **Native Foods**. The health-conscious owner and staff are committed to serving food that is not only good for you, but looks and tastes great, too. The international atmosphere and menu make the best of fresh, in-season ingredients along with expertly prepared tofu and other protein-rich meat alternatives. You'll find tacos, lasagna, "burgers," and even "steak" among the entrées. Save room for the decadent desserts, which include a cinnamon-spiced cake that combines chocolate, coconut, and peanut butter. Closed Sunday. ~ 73-890 El Paseo; 760-836-9396; www.nativefoods.com. DELUXE.

of the beautiful patio, overlooking the passing human parade on El Paseo.

Cuistot
72-593 El Paseo
760-340-1000
no lunch Sunday; closed Monday
DELUXE TO ULTRA-DELUXE

An inviting French farmhouse atmosphere envelopes those who sample the innovative California–French cuisine of this lovely restaurant. During the day, you may wish to be seated on the shaded patio, where a waterfall tumbles over a jumble of boulders. In the evening, tables beckon with starched white linens illuminated by flickering candles. Menu highlights include skillet-roasted veal chops with mushrooms, roasted garlic, and fresh thyme, or poached lobster with baby asparagus and basmati rice drizzled with champagne cognac herb sauce. The premier wine list is extensive and the desserts are a triumph. Try the raspberry *feuilleté* or one of Cuisot's legendary fresh gourmet sorbets.

Keedy's Fountain Grill

73633 Route 111
760-346-6492
breakfast and lunch only
MODERATE

A classic all-American soda foundation and café with a bow toward Mexico, "Keedy's Fix" has been around since 1957, serving dependably satisfying (and high-calorie) breakfast and lunch standards such as omelettes, patty melts, BLTs, and hamburgers. If you dare, try the renowned triple-decker burger with bacon. The shakes, floats, and malts are justifiably famous, and among the well-prepared Mexican dishes are *huevos rancheros*, *machaca* (shredded beef with eggs), tacos, enchiladas, and *menudo* (tripe soup).

Ruth's Chris Steakhouse

74-040 Route 111
760-779-1998
www.ruthschris.com
DELUXE TO ULTRA-DELUXE

The devout red-meat carnivore is well served at this old-school steakhouse, which also does a great job with chicken, seafood, salad, and side dishes. Even vegetarians will leave happy, though their choices are limited. Served in a wood-paneled, low-light gentlemen's club atmosphere, the filet mignons, veal chops, and New York strips are particularly recommended. We're talking about tender, corn-fed, Midwestern beef, cooked to your specification. Besides a full bar, there's an extensive wine list to choose from. Service is knowledgeable and pleasant.

SHOPPING

The region's most elegant stores line **El Paseo**, a multi-block extravaganza that wends through the heart of Palm Desert, between Monterey Avenue and Portola Drive. This dazzling mile of more than 300 exclusive shops, fashionable art galleries, tony salons, and expensive restaurants is often compared to Beverly Hills' Rodeo Drive or New York's Fifth Avenue. Squint your eyes and you could be in Palm Beach. In this glamorous incarnation, the ritzy boulevard is bisected by a landscaped median that also serves as a lovely sculpture garden. As you browse, be aware that in addition to those fronting El

Aerie Sculpture Garden and Gallery

Sculptor-painter Clonard Thomas and her husband, Bruce, invite visitors by appointment only to their unusual 20-acre home on a hill. The arid grounds, extensively planted in desert cacti and native trees, are softened by the trill of recirculating water features that include a small stream and several fountains. One pool is frequented by rare bighorn sheep who drop by regularly to slake their thirst. Three carefully landscaped acres showcase striking sculptures by local artists as well as Clonard Thomas, whose work has been created and displayed here for many years. The sculpture on exhibit is intended to fit in with the garden's overarching theme of harmony with nature. A 1930s homestead cabin contains one of three galleries on the compound that feature the paintings, photographs, and smaller sculptures of various Coachella Valley artists. Serious inquiries only; call ahead to make arrangements. Closed June through October. ~ 71-225 Aerie Drive; 760-568-6366.

BORDERS.

BORDERS
BOOKS AND MUSIC
1212 S. WASHINGTON ST.
N. ATTELBORO, MA 02760
508-699-7766

STORE: 0202   REG: 03/43 TRAN#: 0967
SALE   09/17/2011 EMP: 00075

WEEK AT AIRPORT
    3117967 QP T   1.50
  15.00 90% PROMO
HIDDEN ESCAPES PALM SPRINGS
    7622422 QP T   1.49
  14.95 90% PROMO

        Subtotal   2.99
        MASS 6.25%   .19
2 Items   Total   3.18
        CASH   10.20
        Cash Change Due 7.02

You Saved $26.96

09/17/2011 09:00PM

ALL SALES FINAL
NO RETURNS/EXCHANGES

Exchanges of opened audio books, music, videos, video games, software and electronics will be permitted subject to the same time periods and receipt requirements as above and can be made for the same item only.

Periodicals, newspapers, comic books, food and drink, eBooks and other digital downloads, gift cards, return gift cards, items marked "non-returnable," "final sale" or the like and out-of-print, collectible or pre-owned items cannot be returned or exchanged.

Returns and exchanges to a Borders, Borders Express or Waldenbooks retail store of merchandise purchased from Borders.com may be permitted in certain circumstances. See Borders.com for details.

BORDERS.

Returns

Returns of merchandise purchased from a Borders, Borders Express or Waldenbooks retail store will be permitted only if presented in saleable condition accompanied by the original sales receipt or Borders gift receipt within the time periods specified below. Returns accompanied by the original sales receipt must be made within 30 days of purchase and the purchase price will be refunded in the same form as the original purchase. Returns accompanied by the original Borders gift receipt must be made within 60 days of purchase and the purchase price will be refunded in the form of a return gift card.

Exchanges of opened audio books, music, videos, video games, software and electronics will be permitted subject to the same time periods and receipt requirements as above and can be made for the same item only.

Periodicals, newspapers, comic books, food and drink, eBooks and other digital downloads, gift cards, return gift cards, items marked "non-returnable," "final sale" or the like and out-of-print, collectible or pre-owned items cannot be returned or exchanged.

PICTURE-PERFECT
Art Galleries

1. **CODA Gallery,** *p. 154*
2. **Edenhurst Gallery,** *p. 155*
3. **Heather James Art & Antiquities,** *p. 154*

Paseo, there are dozens of shops tucked into multilevel arcades and courtyards that the casual visitor tends to overlook. Familiar names are here, such as Williams Sonoma, Saks 5th Avenue, and Tiffany, along with many one-of-a-kind gems. Take time to explore, and you'll find something wonderful and unexpected on every block. Many stores give away helpful indexed shopping guides. For your convenience, the city-sponsored **Shopper Hopper** provides a looping courtesy shuttle service along El Paseo, and from several nearby shopping areas and hotels. ~ 877-735-7273; www.elpaseo.com.

Among the many fine galleries lining El Paseo is **San Soucie Art Glass Studios.** Here master artisans have been turning out custom sandblasted glass art since 1976. Pick up a set of handcrafted glass doors, etched windows, mirrors, tables, or sculptures. Closed Sunday; open Saturday by appointment. ~ 73-890 El Paseo; 760-340-3000; www.sanssoucie.com.

Antique collectors with sophisticated taste should be impressed by the top-drawer items on display at **Classic Consignment Company,** where local celebrities are said to buy and sell their cherished wares, presumably as

trends in design and interior decorating change. Five-
and even six-figure price tags aren't unusual here, but you
can find furnishings and accessories at much lower costs
as well. ~ 73847 El Paseo; 760-568-4948.

An excellent example of the several specialized home
furnishing stores on the street is **Between the Sheets**, a
haven for those who appreciate fine bedding and household linens. Ask to run your fingers along the silky-soft,
high thread-count cotton sheets, or admire the fashionable tablecloths and yummy bath towels. ~ 73515 El
Paseo; 760-770-8500.

While visiting the Living Desert Nature Park, stop by
Plaza Gifts, near the main entrance, to peruse its excellent collection of books, prints, and gift items, all relat-

Art Under the Stars

On the evening of the first Thursday of each month, from October through May, the **Art Walk** from 5 p.m. to 9 p.m. encourages El Paseo visitors to visit the promenade's numerous galleries, antique stores, and design studios, many of which stay open late, hold exhibitions, present their artists, and provide complimentary refreshments. In a city where there's precious little "street life," this fun and friendly event is a godsend. The Art Walk also extends to **The Art Place**, an eclectic blend of more than a dozen galleries and design studios. If a month's first Thursday falls on a major holiday, Art Walk is held the following Friday evening. ~ 41-801 Corporate Way; 760-776-2268; www.cityofpalmdesert.org.

ing to the desert environment and many of them suitable for young people of all ages. Call ahead for hours, which are shortened during the summer. ~ 47-900 Portola Avenue; 760-346-5694; www.livingdesert.org.

Extremely popular with both residents and visitors, the **College of the Desert Street Fair** takes place on weekend mornings year-round in the palm-shaded parking lots of the College of the Desert campus. The event, which benefits the school's scholarship program through an alumni association, is spread over several acres and demands a few hours to see everything. Unlike a traditional flea market, the products sold here are new and range from fine art to clothing, furniture to beauty products, gift items to sports equipment. If you happen to need a new birdhouse or putting iron, you'll probably find it here. There are farmers' market and nursery sections as well as an extensive craft area and stomach-satisfying food court. Live music and free parking further sweeten the deal. Open 7 a.m. to noon June through September,

Text continued on page 156.

El Paseo

Try to time your stroll to one of the Friday evenings (5 p.m. to 9 p.m.) from October through April when Palm Desert celebrates Art Walk, during which local retailers and restaurants join the city in promoting its growing arts community. Yes, the El Paseo area is a shopper's paradise, but it's also one of the few places in this car-oriented community where strolling is not only possible, it's actively encouraged and exceptional pleasant. And, there's more to see than simply merchandise.

Start off with something unexpected in this chic shopping district by parking your car on Monterey Avenue (Route 74), a block or two south of El Paseo, and then wander north through one of Palm Desert's prettiest (and most exclusive) residential areas. In contrast to the low-slung desert modern or California ranch styles that predominate in this region, many of the homes on side streets south of El Paseo (Ocotillo Drive and Sage Lane are others you may wish to visit) recall the pleasing country architecture of northern Italy or southern France, with some Spanish mission revival thrown in. En route, make sure you stop at **Imago Galleries**, which showcases fine contemporary art in a beautiful landmark building. Feeling and looking more like a museum than a gallery, you'll see some of the best work by renowned artists Dale Chihuly, Fernando Botero, Tom Wesselmann, Donald Sultan, and Peter Halley. ~ 45450 Monterey Drive; 760-776-9890.

Continuing north on Monterey, at its intersection with El Paseo you'll arrive at **El Paseo Collection**, a cluster of two dozen galleries, boutiques, restaurants and specialty shops housed in an attractive two-story complex along both sides of the street. Galleries worth your time here include **Heather James Art & Antiquities**, featuring ethnographic, tribal, and cultural art from Africa, Asia, and the pre-Columbian Americas (760-346-8926; www.heatherjames.com); **CODA Gallery**, a showcase of contemporary paintings, sculpture, and mixed media by the likes of Chris Young and Donald Allan (760-346-4661; www.codagallery.com); and **S.R. Brennan Gallery of Fine Art**, with a focus on European paintings and sculptures as well as 19th- and 20th-century American painters (760-773-9554; www.srbrennangalleries.com). ~ 73-080 El Paseo; 760-341-9424.

Browse to your heart's content, then proceed east on El Paseo, taking time to admire the great variety of public sculpture on display in the traffic median. Often overlooked by casual visitors, the works (all by accomplished artists) are by turns dramatic, whimsical, abstract, and representational. Mexico City artist Heriberto Juárez's "Caballo con Jinete" is a realistic bronze of a horseman and rider, for example, while Dutch-born Jon Krawczyk has contributed a metal abstraction aptly titled "Flotsam/Jetsam." Some of these sculptors show their work at **Tré Contemporary**, a multi-

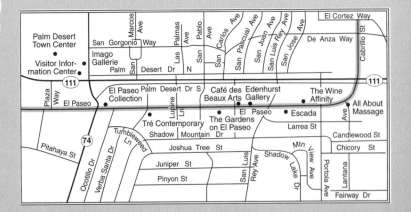

media fine art gallery (a block east of El Paseo Collection) owned by local painters Eric Johnson and Tom Gardner. ~ 73-199 El Paseo; 760-568-2010.

Proceed two blocks east to **The Gardens on El Paseo**, between San Pablo Avenue and Larkspur Lane. This is another intriguing multilevel warren of four dozen specialty restaurants and retailers, including clothing boutiques and art galleries. Enjoy the lush gardens and artful water features tucked away within the tranquil courtyards of this hidden gem. ~ 73-545 El Paseo; 760-862-1990; www.thegardensonelpaseo.com.

Feeling hungry? Consider **Café des Beaux Arts** across from the Gardens at Larkspur and El Paseo, a classic French bistro with great French–Mediterranean cuisine in an upbeat Parisian atmosphere. Dine indoors or on the patio. The chicken crêpes, rack of lamb, and crème brûlée are all delicious. ~ 73-640 El Paseo; 760-346-0669.

Continue your exploration east on El Paseo, ducking in and out of such delights as **Edenhurst Gallery**, whose handsome rooms show off fine examples of American impression, early California art, 19th-century European painting, and art of the American Southwest. ~ 73-655 El Paseo; 760-346-7900.

Keep walking past **Escada**, which features high-quality clothes and glamorous accessories for both men and women (73-811 El Paseo; 760-773-0025), and **The Wine Affinity**, one of the best wine shops in the area (73-900 El Paseo; 760-674-2167), to the intersection of El Paseo and Route 111. Here you'll find **All About Massage**, the locals' favorite for home spa supplies as well as classic and hot-stone massages, epicurean facials, and other spa treatments. Walk-ins are welcome, though you may have to come back for an appointment. It's well worth the return trip. ~ 74-121 Route 111; 760-346-7949.

and from 7 a.m. to 2 p.m. October through May. ~ 43-500 Monterey Avenue; 760-568-9921.

Palm Desert's biggest shopping center is **Westfield Shoppingtown**, a large multilevel complex (formerly known as Palm Desert Town Center) with such familiar anchors as Macy's, Sears, J.C. Penney, Barnes & Noble, and Robinsons-May. One-of-a-kind shops include **Baby Blings** (760-340-0512), offering upscale baby-related items such as bassinets and strollers, and **The Flip Flop Store** (760-341-9424), with sandals and offbeat women's apparel. There are scores of restaurants and service providers here too, along with acres of free parking. Customer amenities include a shopping concierge service and a professionally attended play area for children. ~ 73840 Route 111 at Monterey Avenue; 760-568-0248, 760-346-2121; www.westfield.com.

NIGHTLIFE

State-of-the-art and ultra-fashionable, the **McCallum Theatre for the Performing Arts** is the desert showplace for Broadway touring companies, symphonies, dramas, comedians, plays, and concerts. Consistently attracting top-flight entertainment, this plush 1127-seat theater is

Hollywood Vets

At the **Cinémas Palme d'Or**, a multiscreen movie complex in the Westfield shopping center, live stage shows are occasionally presented by local theater groups. The actors and behind-the-scenes talent often include distinguished veterans of TV, film, and theater who live here full- or part-time. Check local newspapers or ask your hotel concierge about current productions. ~ 72840 Route 111; 760-836-3003, 888-240-3003.

the cultural capital of the entire Palm Springs area, with most events scheduled from October through April. ~ 73-000 Fred Waring Drive, on the campus of College of the Desert; 760-340-2787 (box office), fax 760-341-9508; www.mccallumtheatre.com.

McCallum Theatre for the Performing Arts

Some of the best jump blues, swing, and jazz in the area can be heard most nights in the bar at **Sullivan's Steakhouse**, where the perfect martinis are as cool as the combos. There's also a great selection of wine, beer, and cigars. ~ 73505 El Paseo; 760-341-3560.

Other popular live entertainment venues also serve food. **Durty Nelly's Irish Pub** has traditional Celtic music and sometimes rock or country on weekend nights. ~ 72286 Route 111; 760-674-8225; www.durtynellsirishpub.com. **The Jetty** runs the gamut from deejay to calypso and jazz to blues. ~ 72191 Route 111; 760-773-1711; www.clubjetty.com. **The Red Barn** features hard rock, blues, and hip-hop. ~ 73290 Route 111; 760-346-0191. Each of these has a friendly atmosphere along with such amenities as pool, darts, and satellite TV sports.

PARKS

Created in 2001 by an act of Congress that was championed by the late Congressman Sonny Bono's wife and successor, Mary, the **Santa Rosa and San Jacinto Mountains National Monument** preserves areas in its namesake ranges directly south and west of the Coachella Valley. The federal protection of these 272,000 acres followed years of intense lobbying by environmentalists, citizens' groups, and others who feared that rapid urbanization of the basin would eventually threaten surrounding foothills and mountains that had remained largely pristine. Although this rugged terrain—much of

it officially designated as wilderness—may appear lifeless to the casual viewer, it is actually home to more than 500 different plant and animal species, including the endangered peninsular bighorn sheep, whose population has dwindled from about 1000 to fewer than 300 since 1970. Other marginalized animals found here include the desert tortoise, least Bell's vireo, southern yellow bat, and desert slender salamander. The monument ensures that suitable habitat will remain for these species, while simultaneously providing miles of trails for hikers, bicyclists, and equestrians. The vast park extends through five distinct life zones, from the Sonoran Desert to the Arctic alpine, as it rises in elevation from a mere 300 feet above sea level to nearly 11,000 feet. Those exploring the monument on foot, bike, or horseback are rewarded with sweeping views of southeastern California as well as hidden canyons in which spring-watered palm trees, sycamores, and cottonwoods flourish. Among perennial waterfalls and dilapidated old mine shafts, one may come upon petroglyphs, shrines, and rock structures left by the Cahuilla Indians, who spent at least 3000 years on lands enclosed by the monument's borders before relocating permanently to the valley in the late 19th century.

Santa Rosa and San Jacinto Mountains National Monument represents a new conservation management model in which several government agencies are cooperating with an Indian tribe (the Agua Caliente) and various private landowners in managing a precious resource for the public good. More than half of the property, however, is still owned by the federal Bureau of Land Management and the National Forest Service; and the BLM's Palm Springs office handles most day-to-day operations. You can pick up trail maps and learn more at the park's fully staffed visitors center in Palm Desert. ~ 51-500 Route 74, Palm Desert; 760-862-9984; www.ca. blm/gov/palmsprings/santarosa.

Indian Wells

Calling itself "the desert's premier oasis," this well-manicured city takes pride in its million-dollar resorts, spas, fairways, and tennis facilities (including the stunning Indian Wells Tennis Gardens, where you can see the Williams sisters play and Luciano Pavarotti sing). Not a big proponent of retail development, the municipal government is content to make life pleasant for the well-heeled who live—and visit—what was once a dusty Cahuilla Indian village and later a humble watering stop on the Bradshaw Trail stagecoach run. As early as 1823, the name Indian Wells was documented in the diary of José Romero, a Mexican captain sent to find a route through San Gorgonio Pass between Los Angeles and Tucson. Today, as then, the views of the nearby mountains are lovely, and they can be yours for absolutely nothing. Take a walk or drive; that's still free, too.

SIGHTS

Small in size and limited in public amenities, Indian Wells is a community most visitors—unless they're staying here or taking advantage of its impressive golf and tennis facilities—simply drive through on the way to somewhere else. There is one noteworthy exception, however.

Dwight D. Eisenhower, the celebrated World War II U.S. Army general who served as president from 1953 to 1961, loved to relax and play golf in the Coachella Valley and his presence is particularly remembered in Indian Wells, where he had a part-time home. The **Eisenhower**

Walk of Honor, built to memorialize Congressional Medal of Honor recipients, is located on the south side of City Hall in a peaceful park-like setting with meandering walkways, shade trees, and colorful flowers. The centerpiece of the 5,000-square-foot monument is a recirculating water fountain, which exemplifies the uninterrupted flow of sacrifice that men and women of the armed forces have made for their country. Facing this is an oversized bronze bust of Eisenhower's upper body, shown saluting the eternal well and those whose valor it represents. The Eisenhower sculpture is set upon a granite pentagon-shaped base and is lined by five flags representing each branch of the armed services. Two plaques placed adjacent to the bust describe Eisenhower's accomplishments as a general and as Supreme Allied Commander during World War II as well as his service as president. Immediately to the west is a seven-foot-high granite wall on which are incised the names of several

hundred Indian Wells residents who've served in the U.S. military. ~ 44-950 Eldorado Drive at Route 111; 760-346-2489.

LODGING

Hyatt Grand Champions Resort

44-600 Indian Wells Lane
760-341-1000, 800-554-9288
www.grandchampions.hyatt.com
479 rooms
ULTRA-DELUXE

Comfort, service, and luxury are the watchwords on this 34-acre compound, which added a huge modern spa in 2003. If you need anything, your assigned butler will take care of it. As at other area mega-resorts, the swimming zone has the look and feel of a waterpark, with five separate pools and three hot tubs. You are steps away from championship fairways and tennis courts, along with boutiques, restaurants, a gym, a kids' play area, and other amenities. The split-level guest rooms are spacious and beautifully furnished, or rent yourself a suite, penthouse, or villa.

Indian Wells Resort Hotel

76-661 Route 111
760-345-6466, 800-248-3220, fax 760-772-5083
www.indianwellsresort.com, e-mail info@indianwellsresort.com
128 rooms
MODERATE TO ULTRA-DELUXE

A bit simpler and more relaxed but no less stylish than its mammoth neighbors, this older, European boutique-style resort has a gorgeous pool, soothing hot tubs, superlative service, on-site tennis courts, and walkable access to three nearby championship golf courses. Con-

Golf Resort at Indian Wells

tinental breakfasts and happy-hour refreshments are complimentary. The rooms are spacious, well-appointed, and some offer eye-pleasing views of the landscaped grounds. Suites are available, including one that occupies 4500 square feet. Service is friendly and professional, with more personal attention than you might receive at a mega-hotel.

Miramonte Resort and Spa

45-000 Indian Wells Lane
760-341-2200, 800-237-2926
www.miramonteresort.com, e-mail info@miramonteresort.com
239 rooms
ULTRA-DELUXE

This manicured Tuscanesque property, formerly the Erawan Garden, stresses old-world charm and personal-

Miramonte Resort and Spa

ized service. Families are welcome and even pets are allowed, with minimal restrictions. There's a highly regarded restaurant, a large swimming pool, 24-hour room service, and other amenities. Rooms are spacious and appointed with such details as wrought-iron bed frames, original art, refrigerators, and marble vanity counters. The owners reportedly spent $25 million on a 1998 upgrade, adding a cobblestone driveway and an imposing lobby while also remodeling guest rooms.

Renaissance Esmeralda Resort and Spa

44-400 Indian Wells Lane
760-773-4444, 800-552-4386, fax 760-773-9250
www.renaissancehotels.com
582 rooms
DELUXE TO ULTRA-DELUXE

Despite its being one of the biggest and most modern hostelries in the area, this Mediterranean-style resort somehow manages to keep its atmosphere welcoming, personal, and human-scaled, though its appeal seems primarily to the golfer or business traveler. It's a luxurious, multistoried, and highly ornamented place, with guest rooms that each have travertine vanities, private balconies, separate sitting areas, sunset-inspired color schemes, and two TV sets. In the imposing eight-story atrium, a faux stream flows outside into cascading pools and lakes, while Canary Island palm fronds flutter in the breeze. One of the several swimming pools even has a sandy beach. Naturally, there are restaurants, chaperoned children's activities, tennis courts, a spa, a health club, and access to two adjacent 18-hole golf courses designed by Ted Robinson.

Mangia, Mangia!

Popular with both local and visiting gourmands, **Sirocco** is widely considered to be one of the best (and prettiest) hotel-based restaurants in the Coachella Valley. Named for the hot wind that sweeps out of the Sahara into Italy, Sirocco presents the Massignani family's innovative and classic Mediterranean cuisine, ranging from gazpacho to paella to veal chop Milanese. Celebrity chefs sometimes hold special events in this lovely space, for which you'll want to dress up a bit. Lunch on weekdays only. ~ Renaissance Esmeralda Resort, 44-400 Indian Wells Lane; 760-773-4444. ULTRA-DELUXE.

DINING

Le St. Germain
74-985 Route 111 at Cook Street
760-773-6511
dinner only
DELUXE TO ULTRA-DELUXE

Exquisite Nouvelle French and California-style continental cuisine dominate the menu at this sumptuous
low-key restaurant, which enjoys a fiercely loyal following among local residents. Typical items include steamed
mussels, sautéed foie gras, seared duck breast, and sword-
fish steak. Fresh seafood, imaginatively prepared, is a specialty. You can dine on a lovely outdoor patio (it's cooled
or heated, depending on conditions) or in the elegant
dining room. There's an impressive wine cellar and a full
bar, with piano music most evenings.

NIGHTLIFE

The Indian Wells Resort Hotel, Miramonte Resort,
Renaissance Esmeralda Resort, and Hyatt Grand Cham-
pions Resort each offer live entertainment most evenings.
At **Jake's Lounge**, for instance, in the Indian Wells Resort
Hotel, you can enjoy piano standards or dance to jazz com-
bos Wednesday through Saturday evenings. Band-leader
Tony Carmen is featured during high season. ~ 76-661
Route 111; 760-345-6466; www.indianwellsresort.com.

Join the locals who flock to Renaissance Esmeralda
Resort's **Las Estrellas Lounge** for nightly soft jazz and
dancing or have a drink and enjoy the magnificent
mountain views. ~ 44-400 Indian Wells Lane; 760-773-
4444; www.renaissancehotels.com.

Another option is **The Nest**, a venerable yet friendly French–Italian restaurant and nightclub with a variety of live music and dancing. ~ 75-188 Route 111; 760-346-2314; www.thenestindianwells.com.

So You Want to Live Here

Spend any time at all in the Coachella Valley and you'll hear some variation on this story. John and Jane come here on a winter vacation, perhaps in connection with a conference or business event scheduled at a posh resort. They fall in love with everything

that makes the area special: balmy climate, relaxed lifestyle, fabulous shopping, great restaurants, and an abundance of golf, swimming, and tennis. After another visit or two, they decide to rent a couple of weeks in a time-share, or even buy a condo of their own. Before long, they are part-time residents. After they retire or arrange work here, they pur-

chase a home. At each step of this process, hundreds of options present themselves, including exclusive residential communities associated with private golf clubs. Scores of real estate brokers and property management companies are available here, or you can search ads posted online or in local newspapers. In early 2005, unfurnished two-bedroom area condos were typically renting for about $1300 a month and selling for $250,000 and up. A 2-bedroom house? Expect to pay from $300,000 to well over $1 million. Prices are highest in Indian Wells, La Quinta, and Rancho Mirage, lower in Indio, Cathedral City, Palm Desert, and Palm Springs.

La Quinta   This quiet city's name derives from the Spanish term for "fifth," which took on new meaning when used by early explorers, who often traveled for four consecutive days before resting on the fifth. Over time, "la quinta" became synonymous with a resting place or a place of retreat in the countryside. Point Happy, a rocky outcropping near the intersection of Washington Street and Route 111, was once a travelers' watering hole and the original "resting place" of La Quinta.

Besides golf courses and a mega-resort, visitors will find a boutique-oriented shopping area in Olde Towne, miles of hiking and biking trails leading into nearby mountains, and one of the nation's most prestigious art fairs, held every March. Just south of the city is the day-use Lake Cahuilla County Park.

Tree-shaded, 18-acre **La Quinta Park** in the downtown "village" area is a pleasant place to stop for a walk, eat a picnic lunch, or take a breather while you're visiting, or perhaps doing business at the adjacent La Quinta Civic Center. ~ Eisenhower Drive and Avenida Montezuma.

For information about local activities and events, contact the **La Quinta Chamber of Commerce.** ~ 78-495 Calle Tampico; 760-564-3199; www.laquintachamberof commerce.com.

LODGING

La Quinta Resort & Club
49-499 Eisenhower Drive
760-564-4111, 800-598-3828, fax 760-564-5768
www.laquintaresort.com, e-mail resinquiry@kslmail.com
884 rooms
DELUXE TO ULTRA-DELUXE

Generations of visitors have enjoyed this, the region's second-oldest resort, which opened in 1926. La Quinta Resort's white-washed, Spanish hacienda–style architecture and decor prevail throughout the 45-acre property, which encompasses separate compounds of rooms and villas grouped around their own pools and whirlpools. At the heart of it all is an expansive lobby and restaurant area occupying the resort's original tile-roofed buildings. Check out the historic memorabilia on display here, in-

Inn-credible

The fancy 13-room **Lake La Quinta Inn**, housed in an Italianate mansion beside an artificial lake, provides an intimate, serene alternative to the region's large-scale accommodations. Each spacious room is tastefully painted and decorated in harmony with a different theme, such as the French Riviera, and some have private outdoor hot tubs. Included in the tariff are complimentary wireless Internet, full breakfasts, afternoon wine and hors d'oeuvres, and Saturday dinners at a local restaurant. ~ 78-120 Caleo Way; 760-564-7332, 888-226-4546, fax 760-564-6356; www.lakelaquintainn.com. DELUXE TO ULTRA-DELUXE.

cluding sketches that Mexican painter Diego Rivera bartered with the hotel for room and board. Nearby you can head for golf (five courses), tennis (23 courts), a fitness center or spa facilities. You'll also find three restaurants, numerous specialty shops, and a conference center. Camp La Quinta slates daily activities for kids and there are miles of jogging and bike paths. Adults can choose from a variety of daily mind-body classes that encompass yoga, Pilates, water aerobics, and stargazing. Staying here equates with getting away from it all, and at the same time having all you need right here.

DINING

Morgan's Steakhouse
49-499 Eisenhower Drive, at La Quinta Resort & Club
760-564-5720
DELUXE TO ULTRA-DELUXE

An accomplished specialist in steak and California cuisine, this popular restaurant is named after the developer and original owner of La Quinta Resort, Walter H. Morgan. It is decorated to recall Hollywood's golden age, when movie stars like Clark Gable and Greta Garbo happily wined and dined here. Signature menu items include cooked-to-order U.S.D.A. prime aged beef, whole baked Maine lobster, and veal specials. Dine inside or on the attractive patio.

Adobe Grill
49-499 Eisenhower Drive, at La Quinta Resort & Club
760-564-5725
no lunch Sunday through Wednesday
DELUXE TO ULTRA-DELUXE

Another La Quinta Resort restaurant, Adobe Grill features gourmet regional Mexican and American Southwestern cuisine that may surprise you with its complexity and subtle flavoring. Delicious seafood soup, fideo pasta, and rich mole sauce are among the high-

PICTURE-PERFECT
Romantic Resorts

1. **Renaissance Esmeralda Resort and Spa,** *p. 165*
2. **Marriott's Desert Springs Resort and Spa,** *p. 144*
3. **La Quinta Resort & Club,** *p. 169*

lights. Don't miss the legendary margaritas, made with your choice of blue-chip tequilas. Original art by Navajo painter R.C. Gorman and handblown Guadalajara glassware enhance the Adobe's romantic ambience. The dining room and alfresco seating area boast breathtaking views of the nearby Santa Rosa Mountains.

AZUR by Le Bernardin
49-499 Eisenhower Drive, at La Quinta Resort & Club
760-564-4111
dinner only; closed during summer
DELUXE TO ULTRA-DELUXE

Created by the team of French chefs and gastronomes behind Manhattan's famous Le Bernardin, this lovely establishment (formerly Montañas) takes an inspired Continental approach to meat, fish, and fowl. Azur is known particularly for its extensive international wine list, sinfully decadent desserts, and unique entrées. You'll be soothed by live piano music in a tranquil, intimate atmosphere. To satisfy a light appetite, sample the alluring appetizers at the full bar.

Hitch Your Wagon Here

Situated part of the way up a west-facing hillside that captures stunning sunset views, the lively and eclectic **Cliffhouse La Quinta** looks like something out of a Western movie set, but has a surprisingly cosmopolitan menu that draws heavily on the Pacific Rim, with some Southwest influences as well. Favorites include New Zealand rack of lamb, ahi carpaccio, and duck enchiladas. Save room for the Cliffhouse's signature Hawaiian desserts, such as hula pie and homemade macadamia nut ice cream. Dinner only. ~ 78250 Route 111; 760-360-5991; www.laquintacliffhouse.com. DELUXE TO ULTRA-DELUXE.

Arnold Palmer's Restaurant
78-164 Avenue 52
760-771-4653
MODERATE TO DELUXE

Touting "all-American food endorsed by the all-American king of golf," this cozy, clubby place could also bill itself as a golfing museum. Historic photos relating to Arnold Palmer and golf's early years adorn the walls, and the menu includes some of Arnie's favorites: pot roast, breaded jumbo shrimp, and traditional meat loaf.

La Quinta Plaza

There's lots of other comfort food to choose from, including pork shank, prime rib, and even macaroni and cheese. A golf course designed by Palmer is just down the street, which explains the steady parade of "Arnie's army" regulars.

Coffee Break Café
78-900 Avenue 47
760-564-0226
BUDGET TO MODERATE

This is one of the few places in town where you can enjoy a high-end meal at a low-end price. It's an upscale diner with espresso, wireless internet, and a full bar. Breakfast is served all day, or you can choose from the separate lunch and dinner menus. If you want something fancier than bacon and eggs, hamburger and fries, or a club sandwich, you might consider someplace else. If not, this is a perfectly decent place to get refueled—and check your e-mail while you're at it.

SHOPPING

As in the region's other cities, some of the best shopping is at the specialty shops located within resorts. Check out **La Quinta Resort & Club** for top-name nationally and locally based boutiques. ~ 49-499 Eisenhower Drive.

Old Town La Quinta is a charming marketplace often compared to the California coastal towns of Carmel and La Jolla. What distinguishes Old Town from other Down Valley retail zones is its emphasis on pedestrian-friendly intimacy and one-of-a-kind stores, cafés, and art spaces. Among the many boutiques are **Cha Cha's Jewelry Art** (La Quinta Building; 760-564-7977), presenting Venetian glass, Taxco silver, African beads, European rhinestones and other unusual items; **Toto Tile Too** (La Quinta Building; 760-564-0013; www.tototiletoo. com), featuring handcrafted ceramic tiles, custom murals, and clay-based sculptures; **Paws & Reflect** (La Jolla Building; 760-564-3833; www.pawsreflect.com), carrying a gourmet line of natural pet foods and unique gifts for pets; and **Things on Strings** (Carmel Building; 760-777-9454; www.thingsonstrings.com), which offers puppets, marionettes, kites, mobiles, and windsocks from around the world. ~ Main Street, between Avenida Bermuda and Desert Club Drive; www.oldtownlaquinta.com.

During the fall and winter season, monthly street fairs take place at the **La Quinta Village Shopping Center**. Besides vendors and crafts, you'll find children's activities, music, and a farmers' market. ~ Washington Street and Calle Tampico.

Art Under the Umbrellas is a series of weekend art fairs held on various weekends from October through December in Old Town La Quinta. ~ Main Street, southwest of Calle Tampico and Desert Club Drive; 760-564-1244; www.oldtownlaquinta.com.

The district's specialty shops, galleries, and restaurants present their own **Old Town Street Affaire** from 5 p.m. to 9 p.m. the first and third Wednesday of each month. Artists and other vendors sell crafts, food, flower, beer, wine, toys, jewelry, decorative items, and more. Live music helps keep the mood festive. ~ Main Street at Calle Tampico; 760-777-9554, 760-777-1770; www.oldtown laquinta.com.

NIGHTLIFE

The La Quinta Resort & Club has nightly entertainment in some of its restaurants and lounges, or you can cruise the growing local bar and club scene. **Kristina's In The Cove** offers nightly dancing and revelry. ~ 78-073 Calle Barcelona; 760-564-4771. **Las Casuelas Quinta** has occasional strolling mariachi bands and flamenco guitarists, with a commanding view of Happy Point's nearby silhouette. ~ 78-840 Route 111; 760-777-7715.

At **Hog's Breath Inn**, pianist Steven Sanders often holds forth in the fun see-and-be-seen saloon of this Clint Eastwood–founded Old Town restaurant. ~ 78-065 Main Street; 760-564-5556. You'll find another popular piano bar at **Locanda Toscana**, a charmingly authentic Italian restaurant that recalls the bucolic country inns of Tuscany. ~ 72-695 Route 111; 760-776-7500.

PARKS

Located about six miles southwest of La Quinta, stark is a good one-word description for **Lake Cahuilla County Park**. It's a human-made lake with dirt banks, very little vegetation, and bald mountains looming in every direction. One section of the park has been landscaped with lawns and palm trees; the rest is as dusty as the surrounding desert. Since the lake is stocked with trout, bluegill, and catfish, most people come to fish, swim, or camp. The park offers picnic areas, a swimming pool, lifeguards, a playground, restrooms, and showers. From May through September, the park is open Friday through

Monday. Day-use fee. ~ 58-075 Jefferson Street, La Quinta; 760-564-4712, fax 760-564-2506.

Camping: There are 65 RV sites, all with hookups, and 85 primitive sites. Fees vary. The park is locked at 10 p.m., so campers need to obtain keys from the camp manager. Reservations: 800-234-7275.

Indio   The oldest city in the Coachella Valley, Indio may be flat, dry, and not particularly attractive, but it has

one homegrown product that puts this place on everyone's map—dates. The only region in the U.S. where the fruit is intensively grown, Indio boasts more than 3000 acres of date palms, producing about 80 percent of America's date crop. Tall, stately trees with fan-shaped fronds, they transform a bland agricultural and bedroom community into an authentic oasis. On irrigated lands just outside Indio, you'll see where many of the country's table grapes are grown, along with much of its winter lettuce. By the way, if you wonder where all the low-paid workers live who pick these vegetables and serve the resort industry, you've found the place. Local attractions include historic murals on many of Old Town Indio's buildings, 15 polo fields, several golf courses, and the glittery Fantasy Springs Casino.

City of Festivals

Indio calls itself "the city of festivals" for good reason. Tens of thousands of visitors arrive here every December for the International Tamale Festival (760-347-0676), a celebration of a delectable corn-based staple of Mexican cuisine, and again in

February for the International Date Festival and Riverside County Fair (760-863-8247), an audacious tribute to the world's oldest cultivated fruit. Other annual events include the Desert Circuit Horse Show (January through March), Southwest Arts Festival (February; 760-347-0676), Cabazon Indian tribe powwows (760-342-2593) in November and March, and the PGA Tour's Skins Game (November).

SIGHTS

Its sunny location and modest prices make Indio a favorite winter destination for RV-based travelers, and its designation by the state government as a special enterprise zone helps stimulate new business. Information about the area is available from the **Indio Chamber of Commerce.** ~ 82-921 Smurr Street; 760-347-0676, fax 760-347-6069; www.indiochamber.org.

The 3,000-square-foot **Cabazon Cultural Museum** provides a snapshot of the Cabazon Band of Mission Indian's history and patrimony, with some interesting displays of basketry and other artifacts along with beautiful

wall murals. Tours in English and Spanish. Closed Monday and Tuesday. ~ 84-245 Indio Springs Parkway; 800-827-2946 ext. 85770; www.fantasysprings resort.com.

Two adjacent private clubs—**Eldorado Polo Club** and **Empire Polo Club**—have joined forces to make Indio one of the world's premier polo-playing locations. Even Prince Philip and Prince Charles of England have played here, in what is considered the epicenter of American polo competition. Spectators are welcome for competitions that take place at more than a dozen fields, highlighted by a series of tournaments in late winter. Or you can bring a picnic and watch weekday practice sessions for free. In addition, concerts and music festivals are sometimes held on the polo grounds. Admission. ~ Eldorado Polo Club, 50-950 Madison Street, 760-342-2223; Empire Polo Club, 81-800 Avenue 51, 760-342-2762.

Shields Oasis Date Gardens is a friendly, unpretentious place to try all sorts of date or date-flavored products: milk shakes, ice cream, cake, confections, sugar crystals, and, of course, several varieties of fresh dates. You can sit at an old-fashioned lunch counter or get your goodies to go. Unfortunately, unless you're obsessed with dates, the most exciting thing about their constantly playing movie, *The Romance and Sex Life of the Date*, is the title. ~ 80-225 Route 111; 760-347-0996, 800-414-2555, fax 760-342-3288; www.shieldsdates.com.

Oasis Date Gardens, a 175-acre working Coachella Valley ranch owned and operated by Shields, offers a close-up look at a date orchard that's been in production

HIDDEN

Desert Culture

The **Coachella Valley Museum and Cultural Center** has informative displays on local history and agriculture, including the date industry. The regional facility, based in an old adobe house, contains an "Indian room" with artifacts from the local Cahuilla tribe and a collection of heirlooms donated by area residents. The museum also displays items relating to Indio's prominent role as a railroad town as well as the building's prior use as a physician home and clinic. A favorite outdoor curiosity is a "submarine," one of the many water-dripping, burlap-draped sheds that cooled sleepers on hot nights hereabouts before modern air-conditioning. Also on the grounds are a blacksmith shop, sawmill, water tower, and old farming implements. Closed Monday and Tuesday, and from mid-June to mid-September. ~ 82-616 Miles Avenue; 760-342-6651, fax 760-863-5232; www.coachellavalleymuseum.org.

since the 1920s. You can sample a date shake and other products at the on-site café and store, or picnic in a shaded garden. For a fee, visitors also may go for a guided camel ride through the nearby desert. **Camel Safari** provides this service by reservation only, October, November, March and May. ~ 59-111 Route 111, Thermal; 760-399-5665, 800-827-8017; www.movielandanimals. com.

Another date grower in the area selling directly to the public is **Indio Orchards**, which specializes in the sweet, plump medjool variety. They also grow succulent pink grapefruit and sell it along with various nuts, fruits, and olives. ~ 80-521 Route 111; 760-347-7534.

LODGING

Royal Plaza Inn
82347 Route 111
760-346-8113, 800-228-9559, fax 760-568-3698
www.royalplazainn.com
99 rooms
BUDGET TO MODERATE

Under the Palms

You'll be offered complimentary dates and cookies when you check in to the inviting **Best Western Date Tree Inn**, situated on a five-acre compound landscaped with cacti and citrus trees. The 119 well-furnished rooms are spacious and include DVD players as well as Internet data ports; some suites are available. A few rooms have kitchenettes and hot tubs. On-the-premises amenities include an Olympic-sized pool, jacuzzi, exercise equipment, and laundry facilities. The continental breakfast is free. Ask about golf packages involving local courses. A nice touch here are the poolside barbecues that guests are encouraged to use. ~ 81909 Indio Boulevard; 760-347-3421, fax 760-863-1338; www.datetree.com. MODERATE TO DELUXE.

PICTURE-PERFECT
Outdoor Markets

1. **College of the Desert Street Fair, Palm Desert,** *p. 153*
2. **Indio Open Air Market, Indio,** *p. 184*
3. **Art Under the Umbrellas, La Quinta,** *p. 176*

Centrally located on the main drag and perfect for families or travelers on a budget, the Royal Plaza offers rooms with the standard amenities, or you can upgrade to a suite. There's a pool, spa, restaurant, bar, and conference center. Ask about golf packages with discounted greens fees. The staff is friendly and will answer your questions about what to see and do in the area.

DINING

Ciro's Ristorante
81963 Route 111
760-347-6503
no lunch on Sunday
BUDGET TO MODERATE

Pizza and Italian dishes are the mainstay of this popular restaurant, which has daily pasta specials like scallops with parsley and red wine sauce, along with such unusual pie toppings as cashews with three cheeses. You'll also find better-than-average pepperoni and veggie pizzas, along with pasta covered with red or white clam sauce.

SHOPPING

Retail shopping in Indio is not particularly special and is concentrated mainly at **Indio Fashion Mall** (Route 111 at Monroe Street; 760-347-8823), a modern shopping center, and **Old Town**, the community's partially revitalized downtown business district. Twice a week throughout the year, shoppers also congregate for the **Indio Open Air Market**, held from 4 p.m. to 10 p.m. on Wednesday and Saturday. You'll find the usual rummage-sale treasures, plus new merchandise, produce, and prepared food. The cool weather brings out more vendors and visitors. ~ 46-350 Arabia Street, at the Riverside County Fairgrounds; 800-222-7467.

NIGHTLIFE

The biggest showplace in town is **Fantasy Springs Casino**, operated by the Cabazon Indian tribe. Besides

big-name and lounge entertainment, you'll find slot and video machines, live blackjack and three-card poker, high-stakes wagering and off-track betting. ~ 84-245 Indio Springs Parkway; 760-342-5000, 800-827-2946; www.fantasyspringsresort.com.

A small operation tucked among horse ranches and polo fields, **Augustine Casino** features slots, poker, blackjack, and other gaming along with a lounge and two restaurants. The friendly staff has helped this casino develop a loyal following among locals. ~ 84-001 Avenue 54, Coachella; 760-391-9500; www.augustinecasino.com.

5.

Joshua Tree National Park

The park is an awesome 794,000-acre sanctuary, much of it wilderness, that straddles several distinct ecological zones. It is only a tiny percentage of the estimated 40,000 square miles of desert in California. The park's northern and western portions, of greater interest to most visitors, are in the Mojave, a high desert. The lower southern and eastern sectors, where forests of Joshua trees give way to scrub vegetation, are part of the Colorado Desert. The park's granite hills offer great sport for rock climbers, while its miles of trails attract day-hikers, equestrians, and wilderness enthusiasts alike. If you're simply driving through, allow some time to inspect at least a few of the 50 roadside exhibits and perhaps walk one of the short nature trails. Desert wildlife here includes golden eagles, coyotes, roadrunners, and side-winders, but it is the unusual plant life that makes this refuge truly special. Besides the park's namesake Joshua trees, visitors will come upon stick-like ocotillo (whose tips blossom with lipstick-red flowers) and white yucca (prized by early residents as a source of natural soap).

On first glance, this desert ecosystem may seen so inhospitable as to defy settlement. Yet American Indians lived here for centuries, with some groups living year-round in the Pinto Basin and others passing through elsewhere to gather acorns, cacti fruits, mesquite beans, and pine nuts. They left behind rock drawings, mortar stones, and pottery shards, which can be seen on occasion. After this land became part of the U.S. in the mid-19th century, ranchers grazed cattle in the western part of Joshua Tree. They were followed by miners and homesteaders before the area became a national monument in 1936. It was upgraded to a national park in 1994 and now attracts well over a million

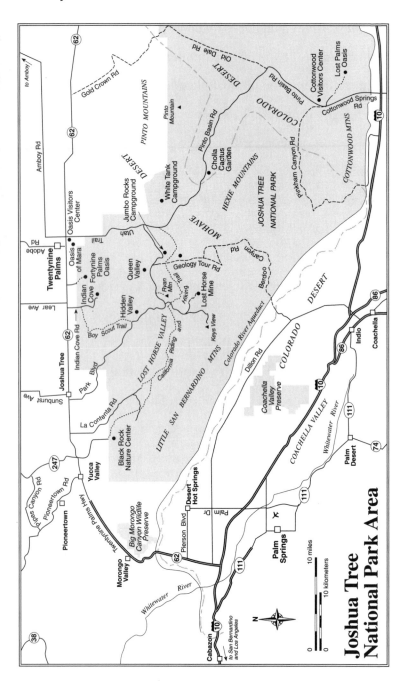

Joshua Tree National Park Area

visitors a year, seeking not only recreation but the chance to enjoy peace, quiet, and starry skies.

At 1237 square miles, Joshua Tree is about the same size as Yosemite National Park, but its road system is simple, with only about 100 miles of paved road connecting three entry points. Facilities within the park include picnic areas, restrooms, campgrounds, four-wheel drive roads, hiking trails, rock-climbing areas, and museums. The most popular months to visit are November through April, when temperatures are comparatively cool (highs in the 60s and 70s) and winter rains spur many plants to turn green and flower. Summer are hot, with highs reaching over 110 degrees and lows in the 70s and 80s. It's always a good idea to spend a little time at one of the National Park Service's three visitors centers, where you can pick up free maps and brochures, buy guidebooks or field manuals, and learn about ranger-led hikes or talks.

On the way to the park's northern entrance you will proceed on The Twentynine Palms Highway (Route 62) as it branches off Interstate 10 a few miles northwest of Palm Springs and proceeds through the Morongo Basin, passing by dramatic rock formations and miles of rolling, sparsely vegetated countryside. Several communities are along this road, including Morongo Valley, Yucca Valley, Paradise Valley, and Joshua Tree, the turn-off to the west entrance of the national park.

SIGHTS

No, that's not a hallucination you're seeing on Interstate 10 west of Palm Springs. Those really are dinosaurs at **Dinosaur Delights** looming above the highway. Or dinosaur replicas anyway. Kitsch and paleontology collide at this low-tech Jurassic Park, where the late sculptor

Geology Lesson 101

Geologists believe the main physical features of Joshua Tree were formed about 100 million years ago when molten volcanic liquid oozed upward from the Earth's interior, pushing a form of quartz-infused granite (called monzogranite) along a maze of rectangular joints beneath the ground. Over time, water and other erosive forces, including extremes of wind and temperature, slowly weathered the hard granite and other mineral-laden rock into boulders, walls, dikes, and blocks, some of them recalling the exaggerated human shapes of British sculptor Henry Moore. Remember, for thousands of years this area was wetter and colder than it has been during the past 40 centuries, so there has been plenty of opportunity for nature's own artistry to occur. Flash floods have caused further erosion of softer rock and sand, resulting in the curious landscape of harder yet often smoothly rounded stone features that visitors see today.

Claude Bell made creative use of concrete to fashion a beloved tourist trap. Have your picture taken next to an apatosaurus (formerly called brontosaurus) that's 45 feet high and 150 feet long, and his companion, a tyrannosaurus rex that stands 65 feet high. Each weighs more than 40 tons and has an interior viewing platform. The apatosaurus even contains a gift shop where you can buy dinosaur toys, novelties, and souvenirs. Bell, who also sculpted at Knott's Berry Farm, died in 1989 before completing a planned woolly mammoth and saber-toothed tiger installation here. ~ 50-800 Seminole Drive at Cabazon exit off Route 10; 760-849-8309, fax 760-849-5900.

Bridging the gap between the High and Low Desert areas along the Twentynine Palms Highway is **Big Morongo Canyon Wildlife Preserve**, a 29,000-acre facility managed by the Bureau of Land Management. This palm-dotted oasis, with several springs and one of the region's few year-round streams, features several nature trails, including a full-access boardwalk that wends through marshes and streamside woodlands. Bobcat and bighorn sheep inhabit the area, which is also prime bird-watching territory. In fact, the density of birds here is

What's Special About a Joshua Tree?

It was pioneer Mormons, reportedly, who bestowed the name "Joshua" on the angular trees they found here during the mid-19th century. Paired limbs of the trees often grow in opposition to one another, like outstretched arms, at the top of a thick trunk. In silhouette such trees looked to the Mormons like the prophet Joshua, in a supplicating pose leading them to the promised land. The spiky trees, related to the desert-loving yucca and agave, are incredibly well adapted to their environment and can withstand long, hot, dry periods as well as cold snaps. Joshua trees are highly resistant to disease and pests, live up to 200 years, and grow 50 or more feet tall. Branching occurs where a flower (fertilized by a yucca  moth) has blossomed and, in general, the more branches a tree has, the older it is. After a tree dies, it may takes a century or more for it to rot, in the meantime providing food and shelter for dozens of other plants and animals while also enriching the nutrient-thin soil.

Drama in the Desert

While in the village of Joshua Tree, stop by the **Hi-Desert Cultural Center** to find out if any dance, music, vaudeville, art, or theater events are scheduled at the time of your visit. The all-volunteer facility boasts an art gallery and 175-seat auditorium, with offerings to the public scheduled throughout the year. Admission. ~ 61231 Twentynine Palms Highway (Route 62), Joshua Tree; 760-366-3777.

said to be about 100 times as plentiful as in most of the surrounding desert. Varying from a cottonwood-rimmed stream to desert washes, Big Morongo Canyon is a place of rare beauty. ~ At terminus of East Drive, Morongo Valley; 760-363-7190, fax 760-363-1180; www.bigmorongo.org.

Yucca Valley's **Hi-Desert Nature Museum** exhibits fossils, rocks, minerals, and American Indian artifacts. It also has an interactive kids corner, and a small zoo with desert animals and reptiles. Closed Monday. Admission. ~ 57116 Twentynine Palms Highway (Route 62); 760-369-7212, fax 760-369-1605; e-mail museum@yucca-valley.org.

Another point of interest is **Desert Christ Park**, a free shrine to peace set on the edge of Yucca Valley. Created by one man over the last nine years of his life, several dozen outsize white sculptures portray Jesus Christ, the Last Supper, and other biblical scenes. A few picnic tables are available to visitors. ~ Turn north from Twentynine Palms Highway on Mohawk Trail and drive a short distance to the crest of a hill, where the park overlooks the town.

A curious local landmark of a very different sort is **Pioneertown**, built in the mid-'40s as a film set intended for Western movies, with backing from actors Roy Rogers and Gene Autry, among others. Between film projects, a few people started moving into some of the falsefront buildings of this ersatz ghost town. You can now take a free, self-guided tour this once-fictional— now real—town, whose structures include a post office, general store, bank, jail, saloon, and bowling alley as well as private homes. Fake gunfights are staged each Sunday (except during winter holidays) at 2:30 p.m. by costumed locals. ~ on Pioneertown Road, about four miles north of Yucca Valley; 760-35-4096; www.pioneertown. com.

Limited water is available at the park visitors centers as well as the Black Rock, Indian Cove, and Cottonwood campgrounds. A good rule of thumb here is to bring

whatever you expect to need, and plan on each person drinking about a gallon of water per day. Dehydration is a real (and potentially deadly) possibility if you're exerting yourself in such an arid, warm environment. Information, books, gifts, food, and drink are readily dispensed at **Joshua Tree Park Center**, a private concession just outside the park's western boundary. ~ 6554 Park Boulevard, Joshua Tree; 760-366-3448; www.joshuatree parkcenter.com.

Black Rock Canyon Nature Center, a ranger station and small exhibit, lies about four miles south of the village of Joshua Tree on Joshua Lane. Closed June through September and Friday morning. This location is a few miles away from the west entrance kiosk on Park Boulevard, which is open year-round. ~ 760-365-9585, fax 760-228-9100; www.nps.gov/jotr.

About 15 miles east of the town of Joshua Tree is the sprawling Twentynine Palms, a stopover with plenty of restaurants, gas stations, and motels near the park's northern entry point. The **Oasis Visitors Center**, less than a mile off Twentynine Palms Highway (Route 62), is a full-facility stop with park exhibits and headquarters. The best place to chart a course through the park, it takes its name from the nearby Oasis of Mara, a grove of palms once used by American Indians and prospectors to sustain themselves. An easy nature trail takes you there in a few minutes. The North Entrance Station to the park lies three miles beyond this point. Inquire here about outdoor classes offered in and around Joshua Tree National Park by the University of California's Desert Institute (760-367-5535; www.joshuatree.org). Variable day-use fee, good for seven consecutive days. ~ 74485 National Park Drive (also called the Utah Trail), Twentynine

Palms, CA 92277; 760-367-5500, fax 760-367-6392; www.nps.gov/jotr, e-mail jotr_info@nps.gov.

Be sure to pick up a park road map at any of the visitors centers before heading into the park. The main paved road through Joshua Tree extends for about 65 miles from the western or northern entrances to the southern one. If you don't make any stops, you can accomplish this transit in less than two hours, passing through several broad valleys and over a few ridges. Several dirt roads, recommended only for four-wheel drive vehicles with high clearances, take you off the beaten path to some beautiful areas most visitors don't see. Recommendations include Pinkham Canyon Road and Covington Flats Road. The former starts at Cottonwood Spring Visitors Center and continues for about 23 miles through the rugged backcountry of Smoke Tree Wash and Pinkham Canyon before intersecting with Route 10. The latter, accessed via the La Contenta exit of Route 62, passes for about seven miles through some of the park's densest stands of piñon and juniper trees, which are only found at higher desert elevations.

If you'd like someone else to do the driving, take a guided bus tour, with plenty of stops for meals, nature walks, museum visits, and photo opportunities. Including travel between Palm Springs and Joshua Tree, such tours last about five hours. Contact **Palm Springs Fun Trips** for details. ~ 877-656-2453; www.palmspringsfun

trips.com. **Desert Adventures Wilderness Jeep Tours** also runs tours. ~ 67555 East Palm Canyon Drive, Cathedral City; 760-324-5337, 888-440-5337; www. red-jeep.com.

As you proceed south and west into the heart of the national park, weathered granite rises to meet you in fields of massive, jumbled boulders. In the foreground, Joshua trees stand tall against a cobalt sky. Many of the rocks are carved, smoothed, and hollowed to resemble skulls, arches, walls and whatever other fanciful shapes the imagination can conjure. With such an abundance of rock, it's no wonder that Joshua Tree is one of the world's top rock-climbing destinations. Especially in winter, you'll see people all over the park, scaling sheer faces and twisted cracks with chalk-dusted fingers and unexpected grace.

The main park road reaches its highest elevation, around 4500 feet, at **Sheep Pass**, 5.8 miles west of Pinto Way. You can pull over for a nice view of the surrounding desert and stroll among piñon and juniper trees that are notably thick and tall at this altitude. A small group-only campground is here, but no water or other amenities.

A popular photo opportunity on the main park road is **Elmer's Tree**, at Milepost 10 just past the turn-off for Geology Tour Road. It's one of the largest and most

Desert Rambling

For a close look at Joshua Tree National Park's legendary rock fields, head west of Jumbo Rocks Campground on **Geology Tour Road**, a dirt road that wanders for nine miles among stone sculptures, alluvial fans, and desert washes.

shapely Joshua trees in the park, with a parking area for your convenience.

Later, you'll pass **Squaw Tank**, an ancient American Indian campsite named by 19th-century explorers, which contains ancient bedrock mortars and a concrete dam built by ranchers early in the 20th century. A pamphlet available from the information centers will also help you locate petroglyphs, mine shafts, and magnificent mountain vistas in this area.

A paved route branching off the main roadway (Park Boulevard) dead-ends at **Keys View**. Certainly the finest panorama in the park, the vista sweeps from 11,485-foot Mt. San Gorgonio across the San Jacinto Mountains to the Salton Sea, taking in Palm Springs, the Colorado River aqueduct, and Indio. The full sweep of the Coachella Valley lies before you, a dusty brown basin daubed green with golf courses and dotted with swaying date palms.

Drive east to west through Queen Valley on **Barker Dam Road** for a look at some of the park's most compelling landscapes, marked by impressive stands of Joshua trees and large boulders where cattle rustlers once hid. Barker Dam itself is an old ranching and mining impoundment, now used for watering wildlife. This scenic detour is off Park Boulevard, about ten miles south of the northern entrance.

The unique transition zone between the Mojave and Colorado deserts becomes evident when you proceed along Park Boulevard toward the southern gateway to the park. As the elevation descends and temperatures rise, plant life becomes more sparse. Yet here, too, the inherent beauty of the park is breathtaking. **Cholla Cactus Garden**, a naturally occurring collection of several species of native cacti that is a pure delight to walk through, is one of Joshua Tree's prettiest places. The garden's "jump-

Climbing to the Top

Rock climbers are drawn to Joshua Tree from all over the world for the chance to climb weirdly shaped granite formations that have been cracked and rounded by centuries of exposure to an erosive climate. More than 5000 climbing routes have been charted up cracks, boulders, chimneys, and cliff faces. Many of the routes are short and most involve use of anchors that are permanently in place. In fact, new bolts may not be added except through a procedure overseen by the National Park Service

(check with the agency for posted rules). Some of the most popular areas for rock climbing include Wonderland of Rocks, Saddle Rocks (at Ryan Mountain), Lost Horse Mine, Hidden Valley, Hall of Horrors, and Indian Cove. Several campgrounds, notably Jumbo Rocks, are close to terrific climbing areas that even novices can attempt. The many wilderness areas of the park are under special protection that carry some rock-climbing restrictions. Serious enthusiasts should consider getting one of the several guidebooks for rock climbs in Joshua Tree, such as *Joshua Tree Bouldering* and *Joshua Tree Sports Climbs*. A number of outfitters and schools offer guided park-based climbing trips and instruction, though some are closed during July and August, when temperatures can exceed 115 degrees in the park. All equipment is provided and you can complete an introductory course in a single day. Reputable outfitters include **Joshua Tree Rock Climbing School** (760-366-4745, 800-890-4745; www. joshuatreerockclimbing.com, e-mail climb@telis.org), **Uprising Adventure** (P.O. Box 129, Joshua Tree, CA 92252; 888-254-6266; www.uprising.com, e-mail susancram@earthlink.net) and **Vertical Adventures** (800-514-8785; www.vertical-adventures.com, e-mail bgvertical@aol.com).

A Glimpse of the Old West

About two miles north of Hidden Valley Campground is **Desert Queen Ranch**, one of the few outposts of civilization in Joshua Tree. It was named for a nearby mine and built in 1917 by William F. Keys, a former sheriff, prospector, and Rough Rider in the Spanish–American War. Keys raised a family here and remained until his death in 1969, after which the 160-acre homestead was taken over by the National Park Service. Among his claims to fame are serving a prison sentence at San Quentin for shooting a neighbor and starring as a grizzled old prospector in the Walt Disney movie *Wild Burro of the West*. On a ranger-led tour you can visit this ramshackle place, which has a restored ranch house, one-room school, corral, barn, and pond. Advance reservations are required. Closed June through September. Admission. ~ 760-367-5555.

---

ing cholla" are so-named because their spines grab the unsuspecting hiker so quickly. With their soft, bristly branches, the more dominant Bigelow cactus live in a region where half a year often passes without a drop of rain. Just down the road is a thick patch of ocotillo plants that graces a hillside with bright color after rainstorms renew their vitality.

Beyond these waysides, Pinto Basin Road passes through a landscape of more ocotillo plants and friendly looking cholla as well as ubiquitous creosote bushes. Then you'll cross through the dust-blown Pinto Basin to the **Cottonwood Spring Visitors Center**, the southern gateway to Joshua Tree National Park, where there's a campground and hiking trail to a palm oasis. ~ Seven miles north of Route 10, 25 miles east of Indio; 760-367-5500, fax 760-367-6392; www.nps.gov/jotr.

Located on public land at Chiriaco Summit, just beyond the southern edge of Joshua Tree and about 25 miles east of Indio off Route 10, the **General George S. Patton Memorial Museum** commemorates Patton's establishment of the U.S. Army's Desert Training Center near here during World War II. Admission. ~ 62510 Chiriaco Road, Chiriaco Summit; 760-227-3483.

LODGING

There are no hotels, motels, stores, restaurants, or gas stations within Joshua Tree National Park; the nearest services are in the towns of Yucca Valley and Joshua Tree, outside the north and west entrances, respectively. Good sources of current information about what's available near the park are the chambers of commerce in each community: Twentynine Palms (760-367-3445; www.29chamber.com), Yucca Valley (760-365-6323; www.yuccavalley.org), and Joshua Tree (760-366-3723; www.desertgold.com/jtcc).

Roughley Manor
74744 Joe Davis Road, Twentynine Palms
760-367-3238, fax 760-367-4483
www.roughleymanor.com, e-mail gnpeters56@msn.com
6 rooms
MODERATE TO DELUXE

This attractive and cozy bed-and-breakfast occupies a historic two-story stone homestead built in 1928 and known for decades as The Campbell Ranch. There are two rooms in the main ranch house and four in separate cottages equipped with kitchenettes. Decorated in a tasteful New England style, all accommodations have private baths and the in-house quarters have their own sitting rooms. Roughley Manor is located on 25 acres and its grounds are shaded by palm and cypress trees, with a lovely rose garden outside the main house. A full breakfast is included and there's a hot tub where you can relax and study the Milky Way at night.

29 Palms Inn
73950 Inn Avenue, Twentynine Palms
760-367-3505, fax 760-367-4425
www.29palmsinn.com, e-mail 29palmsinn@eee.org
16 rooms
MODERATE TO DELUXE

A desert traveler could hardly ask for more than a rustic family inn in a palm-tree oasis. Located in a natural setting within eyeshot of Joshua Tree headquarters—no

lodging is closer to the park—29 Palms Inn has 12 adobe cottages and four renovated old frame cottages. With fireplaces, country decor, and sturdy old furniture, they bear personalized names like "Ghost Flower" and "Fiddle Neck." This marvelous inn, encompassing 70 acres, was founded in 1928 and has been in the same family for four generations. (Be aware that some readers have complained of poor service.) Amenities include a heated pool, restaurant, and lounge. Continental breakfast is served with some ingredients harvested from an on-site organic vegetable garden.

CAMPING

Joshua Tree has about 500 campsites at nine campgrounds; all except Sheep Pass require fees for use. Cottonwood (62 sites), Hidden Valley (39), Indian Cove

Legends Die Hard

Built in 1950, the pleasant hacienda-style **Joshua Tree Inn** prides itself on its "eccentrically eclectic" Old West decor and spacious, comfortably furnished rooms. The wings of the brick building form a horseshoe shape around a large swimming pool and outdoor lounge area. Some of the 12 rooms are equipped with refrigerators and microwaves. One (Number 8) has the dubious distinction of being the place where hard-living rock musician Gram Parsons, a member of The Byrds and Flying Burrito Brothers, took his last breath in 1973. If you visit, ask to hear the full story, which is too complicated (and bizarre) to relate here. A continental breakfast is complimentary. The owners also rent three off-premises cottages and long-term stays at the inn can be arranged at a reduced daily rate. ~ 61259 Twentynine Palms Highway, Joshua Tree; 760-366-1188, fax 760-366-3805; www.joshuatreeinn.com. MODERATE TO DELUXE.

(107), and Black Rock Canyon (100) are the park's most developed campgrounds; only Black Rock, Indian Cove, and Cottonwood have water. No showers. There are five primitive campgrounds: Belle (18), Jumbo Rocks (129), Ryan (31), Sheep Pass (6), and White Tank (15). Bring your own water to the less-developed sites. All vegetation is protected and you must bring your own firewood. No shade structures or utility hookups are available at any of the campgrounds but RVs are welcome at all locations. There's a 14-day camping limit October through May and a 30-day limit June through September. Back-country camping is allowed by registration within the park, with certain restrictions applied. Indian Cove, Black Rock Canyon, and all group sites can be reserved by calling 760-367-5500 or 800-365-2267, or by going online to www.reservations.npr.gov. All other campsites are first-come, first-served.

DINING

Arturo's Café
61695 Twentynine Palms Highway, Joshua Tree
760-366-2719
BUDGET

A simple, family-run Mexican restaurant that's justifiably popular with the locals, Arturo's is famous hereabouts for its large, not-too-spicy burritos. Try the beef,
beans, and salsa combination on a fresh flour tortilla. For
breakfast, the *huevos rancheros* are recommended. The
ambience isn't fancy, but neither are the prices. It's great
for that carbo load you'll need before heading into the
park for a hike or climb.

Joshua Tree Park Center Café
6554 Park Boulevard, Joshua Tree
760-366-3448, 760-366-3622
www.joshuatreeparkcenter.com
no dinner
MODERATE

Sandwiches are the specialty here, with an emphasis
on creative (and delicious) combinations. Try, for example, the nutty chicken salad sandwich or roast beef and

Café Culture

A true oasis for caffeine lovers, the unpretentious **Joshua Tree Beatnik
Café** offers an amazing array of specialty coffee drinks as well as unusual
teas, chais, and juices. The food is hearty and tasty, ranging from waffles,
omelettes, croissants, and bagels for breakfast to pizza, pasta, hot dogs,
sandwiches, and vegetarian entrées for lunch and dinner. The full menu,
including killer desserts, is available at any time. This friendly dining room
has wireless Internet access and there are karaoke, acoustic, and open-mike
performers several nights a week. ~ 61-597 Twentynine Palms Highway,
Joshua Tree; 760-366-2090, fax 760-366-2090. BUDGET TO MODERATE.

Denizens of the Desert

If you have good fortune during your visit, you'll see one of the Mojave's most threatened animals, the desert tortoise, which has

suffered a 90 percent decline in its population in recent years due to habitat loss and crushing by off-road vehicles. These reptiles are holding their own in the park, where such habitat-destroying vehicles are not allowed. Their comrades include coyotes, bighorn sheep, bobcats, mule deer, ground squirrels, Gambel's quail, peregrine falcons, bats, and lizards. The only fauna that poses any potential danger to hikers are rattlesnakes, scorpions, and two species of spider (black widow and brown recluse). The best advice is to not put hands and feet any place you cannot clearly see, and to let folks know where you're going.

cheddar with green chile peppers. They'll even make up a box lunch for you to take as a picnic or after-hike meal. Standard breakfast fare and burgers are available as well. Note that a percentage of all profits are donated to the Joshua Tree Association, a nonprofit group that supports underfunded visitor services within the park.

29 Palms Inn
73950 Inn Avenue, Twentynine Palms
760-367-3505, fax 760-367-4425
www.29palmsinn.com, e-mail 29palmsinn@eee.org
Sunday brunch
MODERATE TO DELUXE

Very near the northern entrance to Joshua Tree National Park, 29 Palms Inn is a homespun restaurant with a friendly staff; local art and family photos adorn the walls. Situated in a rustic hotel, it serves lunches and dinners highlighted by fresh grilled seafood, steaks, vegetarian offerings from the restaurant's own organic garden.

Index

Dining and Lodging Index

Lodging Services

PHOTO CREDITS

Photographs except those listed below are by
©Margaux Gibbons

pages 19, 26, 27, 31, 41, 79, 92, 111, 119, 122, 133, 167, 183, 184: photos.com

pages 30, 33, 179, 196: Robert Holmes/compliments of Palm Springs Bureau of Tourism

page 121: Arthur Coleman Photography/compliments of Palm Springs Bureau of Tourism

page 109: courtesy of Cabot's Pueblo Museum

page 163: The West Course, courtesy of The Golf Resort at Indian Wells

page 164: courtesy of Miramonte Resort and Spa

pages 168, 171, 174: Mike Wilson/permission from La Quinta Resort

page 202: courtesy of 29 Palms Inn

Hidden Picture-Perfect Escapes Guides

More Americans than ever before live in large metropolitan areas. So when they want to get away from it all, they go to smaller, quieter, more welcoming spots that leave the traffic and other anxieties of big-city life behind. This series zeros in on just those types of charming getaway spots. By dedicating an entire book to a friendly little destination, each guide is able to offer a variety of features and a depth of coverage unmatched by more general guides.

Hidden Guides

Adventure travel or a relaxing vacation?—"Hidden" guidebooks are the only travel books in the business to provide detailed information on both. Aimed at environmentally aware travelers, our motto is "Where Vacations Meet Adventures." These books combine details on unique hotels, restaurants and sightseeing with information on camping, sports and hiking for the outdoor enthusiast.

Ulysses Press books are available at bookstores everywhere.
If any of the following titles are unavailable at your local bookstore,
ask the bookseller to order them.

You can also order books directly from Ulysses Press
P.O. Box 3440, Berkeley, CA 94703
800-377-2542 or 510-601-8301
fax: 510-601-8307
www.ulyssespress.com
e-mail: ulysses@ulyssespress.com

HIDDEN GUIDEBOOKS

____ Hidden Arizona, $16.95
____ Hidden Bahamas, $14.95
____ Hidden Baja, $14.95
____ Hidden Belize, $15.95
____ Hidden Big Island of Hawaii, $13.95
____ Hidden Boston & Cape Cod, $14.95
____ Hidden British Columbia, $18.95
____ Hidden Cancún & the Yucatán, $16.95
____ Hidden Carolinas, $17.95
____ Hidden Coast of California, $18.95
____ Hidden Colorado, $15.95
____ Hidden Disneyland, $13.95
____ Hidden Florida, $18.95
____ Hidden Florida Keys & Everglades, $13.95
____ Hidden Georgia, $16.95
____ Hidden Guatemala, $16.95
____ Hidden Hawaii, $18.95
____ Hidden Idaho, $14.95
____ Hidden Kauai, $13.95
____ Hidden Los Angeles, $14.95

____ Hidden Maui, $13.95
____ Hidden Montana, $15.95
____ Hidden New England, $18.95
____ Hidden New Mexico, $15.95
____ Hidden New Orleans, $14.95
____ Hidden Oahu, $13.95
____ Hidden Oregon, $15.95
____ Hidden Pacific Northwest, $18.95
____ Hidden Salt Lake City, $14.95
____ Hidden San Diego, $14.95
____ Hidden San Francisco & Northern California, $18.95
____ Hidden Seattle, $13.95
____ Hidden Southern California, $18.95
____ Hidden Southwest, $19.95
____ Hidden Tahiti, $17.95
____ Hidden Tennessee, $16.95
____ Hidden Utah, $16.95
____ Hidden Walt Disney World, $13.95
____ Hidden Washington, $15.95
____ Hidden Wine Country, $13.95
____ Hidden Wyoming, $15.95

HIDDEN PICTURE-PERFECT ESCAPES

____ Charleston, $14.95
____ Palm Springs, $14.95

____ Santa Barbara, $14.95

Mark the book(s) you're ordering and enter the total cost here ➱ [   ]

California residents add 8.25% sales tax here ➱ [   ]

Shipping, check box for your preferred method & enter cost here ➱ [   ]

❑ BOOK RATE   FREE! FREE! FREE!

❑ PRIORITY MAIL/UPS GROUND   cost of postage

❑ UPS OVERNIGHT OR 2-DAY AIR   cost of postage   [   ]

Billing, enter total amount due & check method of payment ➱ [   ]

❑ CHECK   ❑ MONEY ORDER

❑ VISA/MASTERCARD_____EXP. DATE_____

NAME_____PHONE_____

ADDRESS _____

CITY_____ STATE_____ ZIP_____

MONEY-BACK GUARANTEE ON DIRECT ORDERS PLACED THROUGH ULYSSES PRESS.

ABOUT THE AUTHOR

Richard Mahler is the author of ten books, including *Belize: Adventures in Nature* and *Santa Fe Memories*. His *New Mexico's Best* won the coveted Lowell Thomas Travel Journalism Award for Best Guidebook and his travel columns in Albuquerque newspapers have received numerous awards. Richard's feature articles have appeared in dozens of magazines, including *Outside*, *Great Expeditions*, *EcoTraveler*, *New West*, *Utne*, *Arizona Highways*, and *Yoga Journal*. He lives in Santa Cruz, California, where he teaches stress reduction and produces programs for public radio when not writing about nature, art, health, and travel.

ABOUT THE PHOTOGRAPHER

Margaux Gibbons attended the Brooks Institute of Photography in Santa Barbara, California, where she studied commercial advertising. Her nature photography has appeared in *The New Key to Costa Rica*. She has traveled extensively in Latin America, and is passionate about protecting the environment, learning to live sustainably, and spreading environmental consciousness.